CHICAGO

CITY · ON · THE · MAKE

Dressing the Beeves, Armour's Great Packing House, Chicago, U. S. A.
Preparando las carnes, Gran carnicería de Armour Chicago, F. U de A.

From reviews of the first edition, 1951:

"This short, crisp, fighting creed is both a social document and a love poem, a script in which a lover explains his city's recurring ruthlessness and latent power; in which an artist recognizes that these are potents not of death, but of life."
—*New York Herald Tribune*

"Algren's Chicago, a kind of American annex to Dante's inferno, is a nether world peopled by rat-faced hustlers and money-loving demons who crawl in the writer's brilliant, sordid, uncompromising and twisted imagination."
—Budd Shulberg, *New York Times Book Review*

"The qualities of Nelson Algren's prose essay on Chicago are those of fine poetry—vivid images, richness of language, economy of form, and most importantly, poetic vision."
—*Saturday Review of Language*

CHICAGO

CITY · ON · THE · MAKE

Sixtieth Anniversary Edition

Nelson Algren

WITH AN INTRODUCTION BY STUDS TERKEL

Annotated by

David Schmittgens and Bill Savage

The University of Chicago Press

The University of Chicago Press, Chicago 60637
Copyright 1951, 1961 by Nelson Algren
Copyright renewed 1979
Introduction © 1983 by Studs Terkel
New Preface, Notes, and Bibliography © 2001 by The University of Chicago
All rights reserved. Originally published 1951.
University of Chicago Press edition 2011
Printed in the United States of America

20 19 18 17 16   5

ISBN-13: 978-0-226-01386-2 (paper)
ISBN-10: 0-226-01386-3 (paper)

Library of Congress Cataloging-in-Publication Data

Algren, Nelson, 1909–1981.
Chicago : city on the make / Nelson Algren ; with an introduction by
Studs Terkel ; annotated by David Schmittgens and Bill Savage. — 60th
anniversary ed.
        p. cm.
Includes bibliographical references.
ISBN-13: 978-0-226-01386-2 (pbk. : alk. paper)
ISBN-10: 0-226-01386-3 (pbk. : alk. paper) 1. Chicago (Ill.)—Description and
travel. 2. Chicago (Ill.)—History. I. Schmittgens, David. II. Savage, Bill. III.
Title.
F548.3.A43 2011
977.3′11—dc21

                              2011024140

♾ This paper meets the requirements of ANSI / NISO Z39.48-1992
(Permanence of Paper).

Each edition of *Chicago: City on the Make* has had a different dedication. Algren dedicated the first edition,

> *For Carl Sandburg*

the second,

> *For Herman and Marilou Kogan*

and the third,

> *For Joan Baez*
> *a conscience in touch with humanity.*

The first posthumous edition read,

> *This one is for Nelson Algren.*

We wish to dedicate this annotated edition,

> *To Chicago*
> *with the Socratic imperative: Know yourself.*

Preface

Chicago: City on the Make, like any great work of art, is both enduring and firmly embedded in its moment. In this book—at once both historical chronicle and love poem—Algren speaks with evocative language across the decades, and yet requires of his readers a certain knowledge of Chicago, its people, and its history. We hope, with this edition, to make this vital work more thought-provoking and pleasurable by explaining and contextualizing some of the scores of references Algren makes to people, places and events central to understanding Chicago and Algren's depiction of the city.

The value of the book is twofold. First, it is a beautifully written expression of Algren's relationship with Chicago. Due in no small part to his sense of having been rejected by his city, Algren's poetic prose has a bittersweet quality, a tone of loss and pain vigorously mixed with beauty and possibility, an elegiac sadness redeemed by laughter. Despite all the lost chances at greatness, all of the failures and mistakes and sell-outs, all of the smallmindedness and compromises with mediocrity, Chicago still captivates with its stunning natural and manmade beauty, its boundless human energy. Yet *City on the Make* is no civic booster's text, and here we find the book's second great strength: its unflinching confrontation with history. Any honest description of Chicago must grapple with the fact that much of the city's history is a compendium of low deceit, smiling hypocrisy, organized crime, political corruption, spectacularly unmitigated greed, institutionalized racism, dehumanizing class conflict, and brutalizing violence. Algren believes, along with Theodore Dreiser, that the artist's first task is to tell the truth, and then to let the chips fall where they may. Chicago has lots of chips, and plenty of places for them to fall—and Algren doesn't back away from the truth.

We hope with this edition to make Algren's art clearer by elucidating the people, places and events he uses to build his textual Chicago. In order to keep the focus on the lyrical beauty and political force of Algren's words and to avoid the visual clutter of footnotes, we have added the notes at the end of the text itself. Many of Algren's references appear more than once, and in the interest of brevity and economy we annotate only the first appearance. We have tried, when seeking his sources, to stick with texts available to Algren when he wrote; anyone wishing to pursue our notes further can refer to the bibliography which follows the notes.

David Schmittgens and Bill Savage
Chicago, 2001

Contents

With heart at rest I climbed the citadel's
Steep height, and saw the city as from a tower,
Hospital, brothel, prison, and such hells,
Where evil comes up softly like a flower . . .

Whether thou sleep, with heavy vapors full,
Sodden with day, or, new appareled, stand
In gold-laced veils of evening beautiful,

I love thee, infamous city!

—**Baudelaire**

Introduction

"**I** love thee, infamous city!"

Baudelaire's perverse ode to Paris is reflected in Nelson Algren's bardic salute to Chicago. No matter how you read it, aloud or to yourself, it is indubitably a love song. It sings, Chicago style: a haunting, split-hearted ballad.

Perhaps Ross Macdonald said it best: "Algren's hell burns with a passion for heaven." In this slender classic, first published in 1951 and, ever since, bounced around like a ping-pong ball, Algren tells us all we need to know about passion, heaven, hell. And a city.

He recognized Chicago as Hustler Town from its first prairie morning as the city's fathers hustled the Pottawattomies down to their last moccasin. He recognized it, too, as another place: North Star to Jane Addams as to Al Capone, to John Peter Altgeld as to

2

Richard J. Daley, to Clarence Darrow as to Julius Hoffman. He saw it not so much as Janus-faced but as the carny freak show's two-headed boy, one noggin Neanderthal, the other noble-browed. You see, Nelson Algren was a street-corner comic as well as a poet.

He may have been the funniest man around. Which is another way of saying he may have been the most serious. At a time when pimpery, lickspittlery and picking the poor man's pocket have become the order of the day—indeed, officially proclaimed as virtue—the poet must play the madcap to keep his balance. And ours.

Unlike Father William, Algren did not stand on his head. Nor did he balance an eel on his nose. He just shuffled along, tap dancing now and then. His appearance was that of a horse player who had just heard the news: he had bet her across the board and she'd come in a strong fourth. Yet, strangely, his was not a mournful mien. He was forever chuckling to himself and you wondered. You'd think he was the blue-eyed winner rather than the brown-eyed loser. That's what was so funny about him. He did win.

A hunch: his writings may be read, aloud and to yourself, long after acclaimed works of Academe's darlings, yellowed on coffee tables, have been replaced by acclaimed works of other Academe's darlings. To call on a Lillian Hellman phrase, he was not "a kid of the moment." For in the spirit of a Zola or a Villon, he has captured a piece of that life behind the billboards. Some comic, that man.

At a time when our values are unprecedentedly upside-down—when Bob Hope, a humorless multi-millionaire, is regarded as a funny man while a genuinely funny man, a tent show Toby, is regarded as our president—Algren may be remembered as something of a Gavroche, the gamin who saw through it all, with an admixture of innocence and wisdom. And indignation.

"The hard necessity of bringing the judge on the bench down into the dock has been the peculiar responsibility of the writer in all ages of man." It was something Algren wrote in 1961, as an added preface to this book. It's a responsibility toward which he had been obstinately faithful. He was open-hearted to Molly-O and Steffi and Margo and Aunt Elly's "girl," who were forever up against it; who were forever in the pokey for turning a five-dollar trick with the wrong guy. (That fee is, of course, absurd today. You must remember his heroines subsisted long, long before inflation.)

He's mail-fisted to their judges, the Respectables, who turn a trick for no less than a hundred G's. So, too, this piece of writing from the same essay:

"We have to keep Chicago strong and America mighty," I heard his Honor proclaim before sentencing the girl with a record for addiction. "A year and a day! Take her away!"

Blinking out of the window of an Ogden Avenue trolley at the sunlight she hadn't seen for almost a year, "I guess I was lucky I done that time," the girl philosophized. "Chicago still looks pretty strong and America looks mighty mighty."

Still nobody seems to be laughing.

What Algren observed twenty years ago applies today in trump. And in this prose poem put down some thirty-odd years ago—and what odd years they've been—the ring of a city's awful truth is still heard. Only louder. As with all good poets, this man is a prophet.

It was no accident he wrote *The Man With the Golden Arm* so many centuries before posh suburban high schools fretted about junkies in their blue-eyed midst. The fate of Frankie Machine presaged adolescent hells to come.

In *Never Come Morning*, Algren gave us Bruno, the doomed young jackroller. How different is he, the desperate city ethnic, from the young black mugger? Law and Order is the cry today, as Algren so eloquently italicized the old poet's prophecy: "The slums will take their revenge." Call it ghetto, if you wish.

Yet I'm thinking of Algren, the funny man. The antic sense is there, of course, in Dove Linkhorn, the innocent hero of *A Walk on the Wild Side.* It is there in

Frankie's colleague, Sparrow, the hapless shoplifter. It's there in Some Fellow Willie, who always looked suspicious because he always suspected himself of one thing or another. It's there in Lost Ball Stahouska of the Baldhead A. C.'s. He was something, that one. Remember when his conscience bothered him because he shoved an in-play baseball in his pocket, though he was unperturbed when cracking a safe with the help of three Chicago cops? As to the latter caper, Stahouska explained, "Oh, *everybody* does that."

Again, you have it. Turning a two-dollar trick is a sin and prickly to the conscience. Turning a hundred-thou trick, that's something else again. Lost Ball, were he around today, could well appreciate the workings of ITT, Lockheed, Penn Central and the late Howard Hughes. Recurring in all of Algren's works—novel, short story, essay, poem—is the theme of the rigged ball game. Offered in unique lyric style, they are memorable.

In his poetic evocation of the Black Sox scandal of 1919, he asks the ever-impertinent question: How it is that front office men never conspire? However do senators get so close to God? Or winners never pitch in a bill toward the price of their victory?

Though today's literary mandarins have treated the man with benign neglect—he had in the past thirty years become something of a nonperson—he is highly regarded in unexpected quarters.

About eight years ago, in the streets of London, I ran into a voluble Welshman. On learning I was an American, let alone a Chicagoan, he bought me a whiskey. I had no idea Americans were so popular with the people from Rhondda Valley. It wasn't that at all. He could hardly wait to blurt out, "You're an American, you must know of Nelson Algren." He proceeded to rattle off, in mellifluous tongue, all the titles of Algren novels and short stories. On discovering that I actually knew the man, he bought me drink after drink after drink. And on a miner's pay, at that. How I got back to the hotel shall forever remain a mystery to me.

In New York, an old freight-elevator man, a small battered Irishman, whose one claim to fame was an encounter with Fiorello LaGuardia, asked me between floors if I'd ever heard of a writer named Algren. He had read *The Neon Wilderness.* As far as I know, he owned no coffee table.

Recently, in a conversation with a woman on welfare, a Kentucky emigré, his name came up. It was she, not I, who introduced it. She had been reading one of his paperbacks and saw herself in it. She had also been having her troubles with the Welfare Department and neighborhood cops. As far as I know, she owned no coffee table.

Maybe Nelson Algren's horses always ran out of the money. Maybe his luck at the poker table was never that good. Maybe he was never endowed by a university. Still, he may have had good reason to shuffle along, a laughing winner. And maybe it is for this small work, as much as for his novels and short stories, he will be remembered.

It has been advertised that in his last years, Algren's feelings toward the city he so long celebrated had undergone a deep sea change: the ardent lover disregarded by a cold mistress had decided to end the affair himself, to kiss her off. He did indeed move away from Chicago, as far east as he could go. His bones do indeed moulder deep in Sag Harbor soil. Yet, this singular prose poem (or song) tells us something else: his heart lies buried, waywardly, somewhere in the vicinity of Damen Avenue and Evergreen Street. His own lyrics have lovingly betrayed him.

The Pottawattomies were much too square. They left
    nothing behind
but their dirty river.
While we shall leave, for remembrance, one rusty iron heart.
The city's rusty heart, that holds
both the hustler and the square.
Takes them both and holds them there.
For keeps and a single day.

—Studs Terkel

1

The hustlers

T o the east were the moving waters as far as eye could follow. To the west a sea of grass as far as wind might reach.

Waters restlessly, with every motion, slipping out of used colors for new. So that each fresh wind off the lake washed the prairie grasses with used sea-colors: the prairie moved in the light like a secondhand sea.

Till between the waters and the wind came the marked-down derelicts with the dollar signs for eyes.

Looking for any prairie portage at all that hadn't yet built a jail.

Beside any old secondhand sea.

The portage's single hotel was a barracks, its streets were pig-wallows, and all the long summer night the Pottawattomies mourned beside that river: down in the barracks the horse-dealers and horse-stealers were making a night of it again. Whiskey-and-vermilion hustlers, painting the night vermilion.

In the Indian grass the Indians listened: they too had lived by night.

And heard, in the uproar in the hotel, the first sounds of a city that was to live by night after the wilderness had passed. A city that was to roll boulevards down out of pig-wallows and roll its dark river uphill.

That was to forge, out of steel and blood-red neon, it own peculiar wilderness.

Yankee and *voyageur*, the Irish and the Dutch, Indian traders and Indian agents, halfbreed and quarterbreed and no breed at all, in the final counting they were all of a single breed. They all had hustler's blood. And kept the old Sauganash in a hustler's uproar.

They hustled the land, they hustled the Indian, they

hustled by night and they hustled by day. They hustled guns and furs and peltries, grog and the blood-red whiskey-dye; they hustled with dice or a deck or a derringer. And decided the Indians were wasting every good hustler's time.

Slept till noon and scolded the Indians for being lazy.

Paid the Pottawattomies off in cash in the cool of the Indian evening: and had the cash back to the dime by the break of the Indian dawn.

They'd do anything under the sun except work for a living, and we remember them reverently, with Balaban and Katz, under such subtitles as "Founding Fathers," "Dauntless Pioneers" or "Far-Visioned Conquerors."

Meaning merely they were out to make a fast buck off whoever was standing nearest.

They never conquered as well as they hustled— their arithmetic was sharper than their hunting knives. They skinned the redskin down to his final feather, the forests down to the ultimate leaf of autumn, the farmer out of his last wormy kernel of Indian corn; and passed the rain-swept seasons between cheerfully skinning one another.

One such easy skinner listing his vocation lightly, in the city's first directory, as *Generous Sport*.

Mountain grog seller and river gambler, Generous Sport and border jackal, blackleg braggart and coonskin roisterer, Long Knives from Kentucky and hatchet-men from New York, bondsmen, brokers and bounty jumpers—right from the go it was a broker's town and the brokers run it yet.

It's still the easiest joint in the country in which to jump bond, as well as for staying out of jail altogether. The price commonly being whatever you have in your wallet. If the wallet is empty a fifty-cent cigar will usually do it.

Indeed, the city's very first jailbird got a pass from the city fathers. An antique stray named Harper was knocked down, under the local vagrancy laws, to George White, the Negro town crier, for a quarter. And legally led away by White at the end of a rusty chain.

When antislavery feeling forced the Negro to let the white escape, George wanted only his two bits back. And couldn't collect a dime. So each night scandalized the darkness by crying his loss instead of the hour. He never got his two bits back, but he made a hundred-dollar uproar over it. Every hour on the hour. All night long.

The joint is still in an uproar. Every hour on the hour. All night long.

When the Do-Gooders try to quiet it down they only add drums to the tumult. The village squares arrived too late for a firm toehold.

In 1835 they declared a "season of prayer" and wrested two outlaws right out of the devil's clutches—yet the devil seemed not to miss the pair at all. So they tossed two harder customers into pokey.

And still nobody cared.

Then they fined a brothel-keeper twenty-five silver dollars, and the battle between the Pure-of-Heart and the Brokers' Breed was joined for keeps. The ceaseless, city-wide, century-long guerrilla warfare between the

Do-As-I-Sayers and the Live-and-Let-Livers was on. With the brokers breaking in front.

Broke in front and stayed in front despite being crowded to the rail on occasion.

Not that there's been any lack of honest men and women sweating out Jane Addams' hopes here—but they get only two outs to the inning while the hustlers are taking four. When Big Bill Thompson put in the fix for Capone he tied the town to the rackets for keeps.

So that when the reform mayor who followed him attempted to enforce the Prohibition laws, he wakened such warfare on the streets that the Do-Gooders themselves put Thompson back at the wheel, realizing that henceforward nobody but an outlaw could maintain a semblance of law and order on the common highway. Big Bill greeted his fellow citizens correctly then with a cheery, "Fellow hoodlums!"

The best any mayor can do with the city since is just to keep it in repair.

Yet the Do-Gooders still go doggedly forward, making the hustlers struggle for their gold week in and week out, year after year, once or twice a decade tossing an unholy fright into the boys. And since it's a ninth-inning town, the ball game never being over till the last man is out, it remains Jane Addams' town as well as Big Bill's. The ball game isn't over yet.

But it's a rigged ball game.

Once upon a time, when Thirty-fifth Street was the far Southside and North Avenue was the limit on the north, something called the Law-and-Order League shut the Sunday beer halls, and the Beer-on-Sunday Party won the subsequent elections in a walk. A horde of horrified Ohio spinsters thereupon counterattacking the halls by praying at the bar rails, pleading with the drinkers to kneel beside them.

There is no record of anyone getting sawdust in his cuffs: this was 1873, and thousands who had come to rebuild the ruins of the great fire were carrying ragged banners crying BREAD OR BLOOD on the streets. Sunday was the one day of the week the working stiff who was still working had to himself. So he just dipped his kisser deeper into his stein, wiped his moustache tidily and ordered another. He knew he wasn't getting any eight-hour day by kneeling for it.

Indignantly then in their hundreds the women marched to City Hall to demand legal prohibition of Sunday beer—and got turned down there cold. Working stiffs and out-of-work stiffs alike booing them gently back to Ohio.

After times had picked up again a Reverend Gipsy Smith, dressed like midnight itself, led twelve thousand black-gowned and black-tied saviors, carrying flaring torches and half stepping in funeral-march tempo to the menacing *boom* of a single drum, up and down the midnight streets of the old Levee.

The piano rolls stopped on a single surprised chord, the little red lamps blinked out together, the big drum called "Come to Jesus or Else," and the saviors cried in one all-accusing voice, "Where is my wandering boy tonight?"

"He ain't in here, Reverend," some awe-struck sinner answered earnestly—and the little red lamps flickered with laughter, a piano roll lightly tinkled a jeer, and the revelry crashed like window-glass with one deep-purple roar.

And roared on all night long.

"We have struck a blow for Jesus," the reverend announced without changing his shirt.

"A church and a W.C.T.U. never growed a big town yet," Old Cap Streeter contradicted him flatly. "Hit's still a frontier town."

Where the gouging and the cunning and the no-holds-barred spirit of the Middle Border still holds as true as rent day.

For despite the Girl Scouts and the Boy Scouts, the missionary societies and the Bible institutes, the Legion of Decency and Lieutenant Fulmer, Preston Bradley and the Epworth League, Emile Coué and Dwight L. Moody, there's no true season for salvation here. Good times or hard, it's still an infidel's capital six days a week.

And with a driving vigor and a reckless energy unmatched in the memory of man. Where only yesterday the pungent odor of stewed dog trailed across the marshes, now the million-candled billboards, weaving drunken lights in the river's depths, boast of Old Fitzgerald, Vat 69, White Horse and Four Roses. Where only yesterday the evening crow crossed only lonely tepee fires, now the slender arc-lamps burn.

To reveal our backstreets to the indifferent stars.

2

Are you a Christian?

It's still an outlaw's capital—but of an outlawry whose colors, once crimson as the old Sauganash whiskey-dye, have been washed down, by many prairie rains, to the colorless grey of the self-made executive type playing the percentages from the inside. Under a pale fluorescent glow.

We've abandoned the neighborliness of the Middle Border while sharpening its competitiveness—to lend it a bloodier, more legal edge than the Middle Border ever knew.

For in the time that Dwight L. Moody went about these streets straight-arming strangers with the simple and terrible question, "Are you a Christian?" the answer was simpler and less terrible than now.

Certainly the thief calling himself John the Baptist wasn't one even though he left a religious tract at the scene of every theft. Even though wearing the ministerial black with the Come-to-Jesus-or-Else collar. For he also wore a bright red bandanna about his dirty throat and never a shirt below or beneath at all.

Either you were or you weren't. John the Baptist wasn't one and the bumboat pirate called Black Jack Yattaw wasn't one either. Nor was Paddy the Bear nor Cooney the Fox nor Duffy the Goat.

Nor Red Jimmy Fitzgerald, who conned Charles Francis Adams out of $7,000, and Hungry Joe Lewis, who took Oscar Wilde for another small fortune in that same unchristian year.

Nor Speckled Jimmy Calwell nor Saffo the Greek nor Jew Kid Grabiner. Nor Fancy Tom O'Brien, the King of the Bunko Men; for he murdered Reed Waddell, the inventor of the gold-brick fraud.

Nor the little monster named Mickey Finn, who openly advertised the horror he had devised for the simple pleasure it afforded him to hear some curious innocent order it with his own lips—just before being spun off the stool and into the alley behind the bar. To wake up with the cats looking at him. If he wakened again in the great world at all.

But the Mick was the last of the true infidels.

By the time Hinky Dink Kenna came along you had to cut in closer to answer the reverend's question. For in The Hink the border apache became a working citizen, a property owner assuming civic responsibilities, commanding a ward-wide loyalty and professing some sort of faith or other come Sunday morning. A hustler's hustler, part philanthropist and part straight brigand, The Hink sought his personal salvation in the ballot box.

Like the city that bred him, he had a heavenly harpist on his bedpost as well as a hustler's imp stoking the furnace: when hard times came he fed and sheltered more hungry and homeless men than all the Gold Coast archangels put together. And felt frankly outraged when the archangels accused him of trading free lunches for votes at his Workingman's Exchange.

He'd paid fifty cents in cold cash for every vote he'd bought, he let the archangels know—but what about the missions that were buying blackened souls in exchange for blacker coffee and the easy promise of a heavenly throne? Why was it less noble to pay cash here and now? Let the Gold Coast archangels answer him *that*.

Those same pious Gold Coasters who took the

Righteous Horrors at the nightly carnival put on by the First Ward cribs—while secretly pocketing rents off those same terrible cribs.

Yet in standardizing the price of the vote The Hink did more to keep the city running one bitter winter than did all the balmy summers of Moody's evangelism. Not even to mention Lucy Page Gaston's command that the Chicago Cubs stop smoking cigarettes immediately.

Who came out the truer Christian in a hassle like *that?*

For always our villains have hearts of gold and all our heroes are slightly tainted. It always takes somebody like The Hink, in whom avarice and generosity mingled like the hot rum and the cold water in his own Tom-and-Jerries, to run a city wherein warmth of heart and a freezing greed beat, like the blood and the breath, as one.

Somebody like The Hink's Bathhouse John calling on the city, in the name of its little children, to ban the sale of the deadly coffin nail from within two hundred yards of every schoolhouse. Thus earning himself, a buccaneer to his balbriggan underwear, the sanctimonious applause of the *Tribune:*

> By this measure he will drive from the school areas the petty peddlers in death who have been inviting the children to ruin.

Applause which The Bath acknowledged grandly, bowing first to the left and then to the right, in a wondrous tailcoat of billiard-cloth green, lavender trousers,

pink gloves and a cream-colored vest flaring with dia-
monds—to the greatest rogues' circus ever pitched under a single tent.

For all his strutting piety in Lucy Page Gaston's
name didn't stop him for one moment from leading his
harlots and hopheads, his coneroos and fancy-men, his
dips and hipsters and heavy-hipted madams—his "willing hands and honest hearts" as he termed them—to
flaunt their soiled banners at the Annual First Ward Ball.

Out of their dens and out of their dives, out of their
traps and curtained parlors—most of them carefully
masked—The Bath led his willing hands and honest
hearts with his victory over the tobacco trust in his pocket.
And, in the other, plans for a private zoo. What did his
take from the cribs have to do with whose little children
anyhow, The Bath would have just liked to know.

The fact being that The Hink and The Bath were
the first of the big-time operators. Both living on to see
their territory taken over by the business tweeds who
put a stop to free lunches as being unbusinesslike.

The Hink and The Bath being the first to suspect
that appeals to Civic Loyalty were appeals to empty air:
that the place had grown up too fast to be conscious of
itself as a unified city requiring any loyalty beyond that
to the American dollar. "The cult of money which one
encounters here does not spring from avarice or mean-
ness," one European observer put it quaintly, "but making money is the only aim one can set oneself in a city
wherein the dollar is the spiritual denominator as well
as the financial one." The Buck alone lending purpose
to the lives of the anonymous thousands living in

anonymous rows along anonymous streets, under an anonymous moon.

And singing the old crossroads hymns of Faith Everlasting can't help any more, for you can't call anonymous souls to the Lord. He doesn't know who they are.

And the Lord Himself couldn't get some of them that far out into the light anyhow. They'd think Here Comes That Tuesday Night Lineup Again.

You can live your whole life out somewhere between Goose Island and Bronzeville without once feeling that, the week after you move, the neighbors are going to miss your place. For it isn't so much a city as it is a vasty way station where three and a half million bipeds swarm with the single cry, "One side or a leg off, I'm gettin' mine!" It's every man for himself in this hired air.

Yet once you've come to be part of this particular patch, you'll never love another. Like loving a woman with a broken nose, you may well find lovelier lovelies. But never a lovely so real.

Jane Addams too knew that Chicago's blood was hustler's blood. Knowing that Chicago, like John the Baptist and Bathhouse John, like Billy Sunday and Big Bill, forever keeps two faces, one for winners and one for losers; one for hustlers and one for squares.

One for the open-eyed children of the thousand-windowed office buildings. And one for the shuttered hours.

One for the sunlit traffic's noontime bustle. And one for midnight subway watches when stations swing past like ferris wheels of light, yet leave the moving window wet with rain or tears.

One face for Go-Getters and one for Go-Get-It-Yer-selfers. One for poets and one for promoters. One for the good boy and one for the bad.

One for white collars as well as blue, for our museums like cathedrals and our cathedrals like museums, for the windy white-and-blue miles of our beaches, the Saturday night moonlight excursions to Michigan City, the afternoon at the zoo washed into mists of sunlit remembrance by a sudden warm, still rain; and for that night-shaded honkytonk where Sherry Our Shivering Sheba shook the long night's last weary shake to twenty empty tables and one middle-aged pimp wheedling a deaf bartender for a final double shot.

One for early risers, one for evening hiders.

One for the White Sox and none for the Cubs.

One for King Oliver and Louie Armstrong improvising half an hour on end at the old Lincoln Gardens Bandstand, for Baby Dodds and Dave Tough and all the other real-gone senders, sent-for-and-gone too soon, who brought jazz up the river from New Orleans, made it Chicago's music and then the world's.

For the soldiers and the sailors and the far-from-home marines, who'll tell you, no matter where you're from, that it's the most open-handed town in the country for any far-from-home soldier.

As well as for old soaks' goat's nests, backstreet brothels, unlit alleys and basement bars: for tavern, trap and tenement. For all the poolroom tigers in checkered caps who've never seen a cow, and all the night-club kittens who've never seen a cloud.

For white-lit showups, dim-lit lockups and the half-lit hallway bedrooms, where the air, along with the bed, is stirred only by the passing of the Jackson Park Express. For all our white-walled asylums and all our dark-walled courtrooms, overheated district stations and disinfected charity wards, where the sunlight is always soiled and there are no holiday hours.

For hospitals, brothels, prisons and such hells, where patronage comes up softly, like a flower.

For all the collarless wanderers of the horse-and-wagon alleys of home.

It isn't hard to love a town for its greater and its lesser towers, its pleasant parks or its flashing ballet. Or for its broad and bending boulevards, where the continuous headlights follow, one dark driver after the next, one swift car after another, all night, all night and all night. But you never truly love it till you can love its alleys too. Where the bright and morning faces of old familiar friends now wear the anxious midnight eyes of strangers a long way from home.

A midnight bounded by the bright carnival of the boulevards and the dark girders of the El.

Where once the marshland came to flower.

Where once the deer came down to water.

Wheeling around the loop of the lake, coming at Chicago from east and south, the land by night lies under a battle-colored sky. Above the half-muffled beat of the monstrous forges between Gary and East Chicago, the ceaseless signal-fires of the great refineries wave an all-night alarm.

Until, moving with the breaking light, we touch the

green pennant of the morning boulevards running the dark-blue boundary of the lake. Where the fortress-like towers of The Loop guard the welter of industrial towns that were once a prairie portage.

It remains a midland portage. No railroad passes through the city. Passengers shift from one to another of half a dozen stations. Freight trains are shunted around belt lines. But the Constellations overhead begin to lend it the look of a mid-world portage, with all the sky for its ocean-port.

The city divided by the river is further divided by racial and lingual differences. The Near Northside, centering around the comical old humpty-dumpty water tower which survived the fire, is, for example, almost as different from the Near Northwest Side, just over the bridge, in manners, mores, vocations and habits of speech, as Bronzeville is from Rogers Park.

So if you're entirely square yourself, bypass the forest of furnished rooms behind The Loop and stay on the Outer Drive till you swing through Lincoln Park. Then move, with the lake still on your square right hand, into those suburbs where the lawns are always wide, the sky is always smokeless, the trees are forever leafy, the churches are always tidy, gardens are always landscaped, streets are freshly swept, homes are pictures out of *Town and Country*. And the people are stuffed with kapok.

For the beat of the city's enormous heart, at the forge in the forest behind the towers, is unheard out in this spiritual Sahara. Where the homes so complacent, and the churches so smug, leave an airlessness like a microscopic dust over the immaculate pews and the self-important bookshelves. The narrow streets of the tenements seem to breathe more easily, as though closer to actual earth, than do these sinless avenues. Where *Reader's Digest* is a faith, the Reverend Bradley is a prophet, and nothing but Sunday morning services can dissuade the hunter one moment from the prey.

...... 12. East Water St—Commission Houses.

3

The silver-colored
yesterday

All that long-ago August day the sun lay like shellac on the streets, but toward evening a weary small breeze wandered out of some saloon or other, toured Cottage Grove idly awhile, then turned, aimlessly as ever, west down Seventy-first.

The year was 1919, Shoeless Joe Jackson was out-hitting Ty Cobb, God was in his Heaven, Carl Wanderer was still a war hero, John Dillinger was an Indiana farm boy and the cops were looking cautiously, in all the wrong corners, for Terrible Tommy O'Connor.

And every Saturday evening the kid called Nephew and I hauled a little red wagon load of something called the *Saturday Evening Blade*, a rag if there ever was one, down Cottage Grove to the wrought-iron Oakwoods Cemetery gate. There to hawk it past the long-moldering graves of Confederate prisoners who had died at Camp Douglas in some long-ago wrought-iron war.

When we sold out we'd just hang around the gate waiting for Nephew's Uncle Johnson to break out of the saloon directly across the way. The bartender ran us off if we came near the doors without the iron-clad alibi of having a fight to watch, and Uncle J. was the white hope of that corner.

If no brawl developed of itself the barflies were certain to arrange something for poor Johnson, an over-sized spastic with a puss like a forsaken moose, whose sole idea in battle was to keep his hands in front of his eyes. Some white hope.

Uncle's whole trouble, Nephew confided in me as half owner of the little red wagon, was that he had gone to work too young.

Some uncle. We used to hear him hymning at the bar—

Oh he walks wit' me
'N he talks wit' me—

and the barflies encouraging him mockingly.

He was deeply religious, and the barflies encouraged him in everything—drinking, hymning or fighting, fornication or prayer. As though there were something wondrously comical about everything Uncle attempted.

I remember that poor hatless holy Johnson yet, lurching upon some unsaved little tough with a face shadowed by a cap and a lit cigarette on his lip—the cigarette bobbles and Uncle reels back, blood from his nose coming into his mouth. The Cap yanks him forward, feints his hands down off his eyes and raps him a smashing banneger in the teeth. "It's a case of a good little man whippin' a good big man, that's all," Nephew advised me confidentially, holding our little red wagon behind him. Then the soft shuffle-shuffle of The Cap's shoes imitating the White City professionals.

"Finish the clown off," Nephew encourages The Cap softly. That's the kind of family it was.

Uncle had never learned to fall down. He'd reel, lurch, bleed, bellow and bawl until the bartender would break the thing up at last, wiping Uncle's ashen face with a bar towel in the arc-lamp's ashen light. Till the others came crowding with congratulations right out of the bottle, pouring both into Uncle right there on the street. Then a spot of color would touch his cheeks and he'd break out into that terrible lament—

'N he tells me I am his own.

to show us all he'd won again. Uncle had some such
spiritual triumph every Saturday night.

I used to hang open-mouthed around that sort of
thing, coming away at last feeling nothing save some
sort of city-wide sorrow. Like something had finally gone
terribly wrong between the cross atop St. Columbanus
and that wrought-iron gate, out of an old wrought-iron
war, forever guarding the doubly-dead behind us.

No one could tell me just what.

The wisest thing to do was simply to go beer-cork
hunting behind the saloon. With the city spreading all
about. Like some great diseased toadstool under a shel-
tering, widespread sky. Then to haul our little red wagon
slowly home, with Nephew humming all to himself,
"Be my little bay-bee bum-bul bee, buzz buzz buzz."

Maybe the whole town went to work too young.

For it's still a Godforsaken spastic, a cerebral-palsy
natural among cities, clutching at the unbalanced air:
topheavy, bleeding and blind. Under a toadstool-col-
ored sky.

Maybe we all went to work too young.

Yet that was a time of several treasures: one sun-
bright-yellow beer cork with a blood-red owl engraved
upon it, a Louisville slugger bat autographed by Swede
Risberg, and a Comiskey Park program from one hot
and magic Sunday afternoon when Nephew and I hid
under the cool bleachers for three hours before game
time. To come out blinking at last into the roaring stands,

with the striped sun on them. And Eddie Cicotte shutting out Carl Mays.

The morning we moved from the far Southside to North Troy Street I had all three treasures on me. And Troy Street led, like all Northside streets—and alleys too—directly to the alien bleachers of Wrigley Field.

"Who's yer fayvrut player?" the sprouts in baseball caps waiting in front of the house had to know before I could pass. I put the horn of the Edison victrola I was carrying down on the sidewalk at my feet before replying. It didn't sound like something asked lightly.

But the suddenly far-distant White Sox had had a competent sort of athlete at short and I considered myself something of a prospect in that position too. "Swede Risberg," I answered confidently, leaning on the Louisville slugger with the autograph turned too casually toward the local loyalty board.

I didn't look like such a hot prospect to North Troy Street, I could tell that much right there and then. "It got to be a National Leaguer," the chairman advised me quietly. So that's how the wind was blowing.

I spent three days leaning on that autograph, watching the other sprouts play ball. They didn't even use American League bats. "Charley Hollocher then," I finally capitulated, naming the finest fielding shortstop in the National League, "account I t'row righty too."

"Hollocher belongs to Knifey," I was informed—but I could fight Knifey for him, I had the right.

I wouldn't have fought Knifey's baby sister for Grover Cleveland Alexander and Bill Killefer thrown in. And could only think nostalgically of the good simple life of the far Southside, where kids had names like "Nephew" and "Cousin," and where a man's place among men could be established by the number of *Saturday Evening Blades* he sold. I went through the entire roster of National League shortstops before finding one unclaimed by anyone else on Troy Street—Ivan Olson, an ex-American Leaguer coming to the end of his career with the team then known as the Brooklyn Robins.

But Olson was taking a lot of booing from the Flatbush crowd that season because he had a habit of protesting a called third strike by throwing his bat in the air—and every time he did it an umpire would pick it up and toss it higher. No eleven-year-old wants to be on the side of any player who isn't a hero to the stands. "If I *got* to pick a Swede"—I stood up to The Committee at last—"I'll stick to Risberg—I seen him play once is why."

Well, you could say your old man was a millionaire if that was your mood and nobody would bother to make you take it back. You might even hint that you knew more about girls than you were telling and still get by. But there wasn't one of those Troy Street wonders who'd yet seen his "fayvrut player" actually play. You had to back that sort of statement up. I pulled out the Comiskey Park program hurriedly.

They handed it around in a circle, hand to grubby hand, examining the penciled score for fraud. When it came back to my own hand I was in.

In without selling out: I'd kept the faith with The Swede.

The reason I never got to play anything but right

field the rest of that summer I attribute to National League politics pure and simple.

Right field was a coal-shed roof with an American League sun suspended directly overhead. A height from which I regarded with quiet scorn the worshipers of false gods hitting scratchy little National League bloopers far below. There wasn't one honest-to-God American League line drive all summer.

It wasn't till a single sunless morning of early Indian summer that all my own gods proved me false: Risberg, Cicotte, Jackson, Weaver, Felsch, Gandil, Lefty Williams and a utility infielder whose name escapes me—wasn't it McMillen? The Black Sox were the Reds of that October and mine was the guilt of association.

And the charge was conspiracy.

Benedict Arnolds! Betrayers of American Boyhood, not to mention American Girlhood and American Womanhood and American Hoodhood. Every bleacher hasbeen, newspaper mediocrity and pulpit inanity seized the chance to regain his lost pride at the expense of seven of the finest athletes who ever hit into a double play. And now stood stripped to the bleacher winds in the very sight of Comiskey and God.

I was the eighth. I climbed down from right field to find The Committee waiting.

"Let's see that score card again."

I brought it forth, yellow now with a summer of sun and honest sweat, but still legible. When it came back this time I was only allowed to touch one corner, where a grubby finger indicated the date in July of 1920. Risberg had sold out in the preceding September and I was coming around Troy Street almost a year later pretending I believed Risberg to be an honest man. I'd gone out to the ball park, seen him play in person and was now insisting I'd seen nothing wrong, nothing wrong at all. The moving finger stopped on Risberg's sorrowful name: four times at bat without a hit, caught sleeping óff second, and a wild peg to first. And I still pretended I hadn't suspected a *thing?*

"I wasn't there when he *really* thrun the game," I tried to hedge. "It was a different day when he played bum on purpose."

The Tobey of *that* committee was a sprout who had a paying thing going, for weekdays, in the resale of colored paper-picture strips of major-league players. He bought them ten for a penny and resold them to us for two, making himself as high as a dollar a week, of which fifty cents went to his Sunday-school collection plate. I'd once seen his lips moving at the plate, praying for a hit. "What do *you* think he was doin' tossin' wild to first?" this one wanted to know now.

"I figure he was excited, it was a real close play."

"You mean for your all-time All-American fayvrut player you pick a guy who gets excited on the close ones?"

"I didn't know it was for all time," was all I could think to reply. "I thought it was just for this year."

"What kind of American *are* you anyhow?" he wanted to know. He had me. I didn't know what kind I was.

"No wonder you're always in right field where nothin' ever comes—nobody could trust you in center."

He was really cutting me up, this crusader.

"Well, I asked for Hollocher in the first place," I recalled.

"You could still fight Knifey for him."

"I'll just take Ivan Olson."

"That's not the question."

"What *is* the question?"

"The question is who was the guy, he knock down two perfec' pegs to the plate in a world-series game, one wit' the hand 'n one wit' the glove?"

"Cicotte done *that*."

" 'N who was Cicotte's roommate?"

Too late I saw where the trap lay: Risberg. I was dead.

"We all make mistakes, fellas," I broke at last. "We all goof off, we're all human—it's what *I* done, I goofed off too—it just goes to show you guys I'm human too. I ain't mad at you guys, you're all good guys, don't be mad at *me*." Choked with guilt and penitence, crawling on all fours like a Hollywood matinee idol, I pleaded to be allowed, with all my grievous faults, to go along with the gang. "Can I still have Olson, fellas? Can I keep my job if I bum-rap some people for you?"

Out of the welter of accusations, half denials and sudden silences a single fact drifted down: that Shoeless Joe Jackson couldn't play bad baseball even if he were trying to. He hit .375 that series and played errorless ball, doing everything a major-leaguer could to win. Nearing sixty today, he could probably still outhit anything now wearing a National League uniform.

Only, I hadn't picked Shoeless Joe. I'd picked the man who, with Eddie Cicotte, bore the heaviest burden of all our dirty Southside guilt. The Black Sox had played scapegoat for Rothstein and I'd played the goat for The Swede.

So wound up that melancholy season grateful to own the fast-fading Olson. When he went back to Rochester or somewhere they started calling me "Olson" too. Meaning I ought to go back to Rochester too. I took that. But when they began calling me "Svenska" that was too much. I fought.

And got the prettiest trimming you'd ever care to see. Senator Tobey himself administered it, to ringing applause, his Sunday-school change jingling righteously with his footwork. Leaving me at last with two chipped teeth, an orchid-colored shiner and no heart left, even for right field, for days.

However do senators get so close to God? How is it that front-office men never conspire? That matinee idols feel such guilt? Or that winners never pitch in a bill toward the price of their victory?

I traded off the Risberg bat, so languid had I become, for a softball model autographed only by Klee Brothers, who were giving such bats away with every suit of boy's clothing bought on the second floor. And flipped the program from that hot and magic Sunday when Cicotte was shutting out everybody forever, and a triumphant right-hander's wind had blown all the score cards across home plate, into the Troy Street gutter.

I guess that was one way of learning what Hustlertown, sooner or later, teaches all its sandlot sprouts. "Everybody's out for The Buck. Even big-leaguers."

Even Swede Risberg.

4

Love is for barflies

Before you earn the right to rap any sort of joint, you have to love it a little while. You have to belong to Chicago like a crosstown transfer out of the Armitage Avenue barns first; and you can't rap it then just because you've been crosstown.

Yet if you've tried New York for size and put in a stint in Paris, lived long enough in New Orleans to get the feel of the docks and belonged to old Marseille awhile, if the streets of Naples have warmed you and those of London have chilled you, if you've seen the terrible green-grey African light moving low over the Sahara or even passed hurriedly through Cincinnati—then Chicago is your boy at last and you can say it and make it stick:

That it's a backstreet, backslum loudmouth whose challenges go ringing 'round the world like any green punk's around any neighborhood bar where mellower barflies make the allowances of older men: "The punk is just quackin' 'cause his knees is shakin' again."

"What's the percentage?" the punk demands like he really has a right to know. "Who's the fix on this corner?"

A town with many ways of fixing its corners as well as its boulevards, some secret and some wide open. A town of many angry sayings, some loud and some soft; some out of the corner of the mouth and some straight off the shoulder.

"You make rifles," the Hoosier fireman told ten thousand workingmen massed at a Socialist picnic here, "and are always at the wrong end of them."

"Show me an honest man and I'll show you a damned fool," the president of the Junior Steamfitters' League told the visiting president of the Epworth League.

"I don't believe in Democracy," the clown from the National Association of Real Estate Boards reassured his fellow clowns. "I think it stinks."

"I'll take all I can get," the blind panhandler added, quietly yet distinctly, in the Madison Street half-way house.

"You can get arrested in Chicago for walking down the street with another man's wife," the cops forewarn the out-of-town hustler smugly.

"I despise your order, your law, your force-propped authority," the twenty-two-year-old defied the ancient remaindered judge. "Hang me for it!"

And the strange question inscribed for posterity on every dark, drawn shade of the many-roomed brothel that once stood on Wells and Monroe, asked simply:

WHY NOT?

"A lot you got to holler," the wardheeler who protected many such drawn shades subsequently advised the crusading minister. "You live off the people down in your patch too, don't you?"

"If you're that smart"—the hustler put a stop to the argument—"why ain't you no millionaire?"

Cruising down Milwaukee Avenue on any Loop-bound trolley on any weekday morning, the straphangers to Success who keep the factories and the ginmills running stand reading the papers that could as well be published in Israel or Athens, in Warsaw or in Rome. On either side of the tracks are the shops with the American signs in one window and alien legends in the other: Spanish, Polish, Italian, Hebrew, Chinese or Greek.

Between stops stretch the streets where the shadow of the tavern and the shadow of the church form a single dark and double-walled dead end. Narrow streets where the summer sun rocks, like a Polish accordion, with a louder, shinier, brassier blare than American music anywhere. Churches that look as though they'd been brought over whole, without a brick missing, from Stockholm and Lodz, Dublin or Budapest: from all the old beloved places. Negro churches, as often as not, bearing Hebrew characters out of some time when the building was a synagogue.

Yet the city keeps no creed, prefers no particular spire, advances no one color, tolerates all colors: the dark faces and the blue-eyed tribes, the sallow Slavs and the olive Italians. All the creeds that persecution harassed out of Europe find sanctuary on this ground, where no racial prejudice is permitted to stand up.

We insist that it go at a fast crawl, the long way around.

The Negro is not seriously confronted here with a stand-up and head-on hatred, but with something psychologically worse: a soft and protean awareness of white superiority everywhere, in everything, the more infuriating because it is as polite as it is impalpable. Nobody even *thought* such a thing, my dear.

So we peg the rents just a teensy-weensy bit—say twenty-five per cent—if you happen to be a Negro and so can well afford it.

If you're black you'd better afford it.

If you're white,

a Forty-seventh Street minstrel sometimes sings, mostly
to himself,

> Well, awright.
> If you're brown, stick aroun'.
> If you're black, step back
> Step back
> Step back
> Step back.

And no one will ever name the restaurants you
mustn't eat in nor the bars you mustn't drink at. Find
them out for yourself, greyboy. Make your own little
list. Of the streets you mustn't live on, the hotels where
you can't register, the offices you can't work in and the
unions you can never join. Make a good long list and
have it typed in triplicate. Send one copy off to Senator
Douglas and one to King Levinsky.

The King and the Senator are equally concerned.

You can belong to New Orleans. You can belong
to Boston or San Francisco. You might conceivably—
however clandestinely—belong to Philadelphia. But you
can't belong to Chicago any more than you can belong
to the flying saucer called Los Angeles. For it isn't so
much a city as it is a drafty hustler's junction in which
to hustle awhile and move on out of the draft.

That's why the boys and girls grow up and get out.

Forever fancying some world-city right out of the
books wherein some great common purpose lends
meaning to their lives. As no brokers' portage ever can.

So they go to New York and merely grow sharp. Or they go to Hollywood and soften like custard left in the Sunset Boulevard sun.

Or to Paris, the top of the sky and the end of the world, for the special sort of wonder they cannot live without—and find nothing but American pansies packed three deep at the bars and aging American divorcées in summer furs carting pekes around in baskets especially constructed for the peke trade. When the peke-and-pansy season is past they get one fleeting glint of the City of Light like their world-city out of the books—and know, in that swift homesick moment, that they're as close to home, and as far, as ever they'll be.

For Paris and London and New York and Rome are all of a piece, their tendrils deep in the black loam of the centuries; like so many all-year-round ferns tethered fast in good iron pots and leaning always, as a natural plant ought, toward what little light there is. But Chicago is some sort of mottled offshoot, with trailers only in swamp and shadow, twisting toward twilight rather than to sun; a loosely jointed sport too hardy for any pot. Yet with that strange malarial cast down its stem.

You can be a typical Parisian, you can be a typical New Yorker if that helps when the cocktail lounges close. But if you can find anything in pants, skirts or a Truman Capote opera cape passing itself off as a typical Chicagoan we'll personally pay his fare back to *Flair.*

New York has taken roots as deep as the Empire State Building is tall. Detroit is a parking lot about a sports arena. New Orleans is mellow where it isn't sear. St. Louis, albeit still green in spots after lo these many springs, has definitely had it. Kansas City has gone as far as it can go. San Francisco is complete. Philadelphia appears finished.

But Hustlertown keeps spreading itself all over the prairie grass, always wider and whiter: the high broken horizon of its towers overlooks this inland sea with more dignity than Athens' and more majesty than Troy's. Yet the caissons below the towers somehow never secure a strong natural grip on the prairie grasses.

A town that can look, in the earliest morning light, like the fanciest all-around job since Babylon. And by that same night, south down State or north on Clark or west on Madison, seem as though the Pottawattomies had been the wisest after all.

Most native of American cities, where the chrome-colored convertible cuts through traffic ahead of the Polish peddler's pushcart. And the long, low-lighted parlor-cars stroke past in a single, even yellow flow. Where the all-night beacon guiding the stratoliners home lights momently, in its vasty sweep, the old-world villages crowding hard one upon the other.

Big-shot town, small-shot town, jet-propelled old-fashioned town, by old-world hands with new-world tools built into a place whose heartbeat carries farther than its shout, whose whispering in the night sounds less hollow than its roistering noontime laugh: they have builded a heavy-shouldered laugher here who went to work too young.

And grew up too arrogant, too gullible, too swift to mockery and too slow to love. So careless and so soon careworn, so challenging yet secretly despairing—how can such a cocksure Johnson of a town catch anybody but a barfly's heart?

Catch the heart and just hold it there with no bar even near?

Yet on nights when, under all the arc-lamps, the little men of the rain come running, you'll know at last that, long long ago, something went wrong between St. Columbanus and North Troy Street. And Chicago divided your heart.

Leaving you loving the joint for keeps.

Yet knowing it never can love you.

Bathers. Lake Michigan. Chicago.
Copyright, 1908, by Stereo-Travel Co.

5

Bright faces of tomorrow

Giants lived here once. It was the kind of town, thirty years gone, that made big men out of little ones. It was geared for great deeds then, as it is geared for small deeds now.

In Vachel Lindsay's day, in Carl Sandburg's day, in the silver-colored yesterday, in Darrow's and Masters' and Edna Millay's day, writers and working stiffs alike told policemen where to go, the White Sox won the pennant with a team batting average of .228 and the town was full of light.

Now it's the place where we do as we're told, praise poison, bless the F.B.I., yearn wistfully for just one small chance to prove ourselves more abject than anyone yet for expenses to Washington and return—You Too Can Learn to Trap Your Man—and applaud the artist, hanging for sale beside his work, with an ancestral glee.

52

And cannot understand how it can be that others are happier than ourselves. And why it seems that no one loves us now as they once did. No giants live on Rush Street any more.

Since the middle twenties the only party of over-average height to stop off here awhile was a Mississippi Negro named Wright. And he soon abandoned his potentialities, along with his people, somewhere along Forty-seventh Street. Potentialities still lying around behind some chicken shack or other down there, gathering mold about the edges but still too heavy for any one else on Forty-seventh, or anywhere else in town for that matter, to lift. While, rumor has it, he preoccupies himself with the heady task of becoming a Café Flore intellectual. With approximately the same equipment for such a task as Herb Graffis. For the artist lucky enough to come up in Chicago there ought to be a warning engraved on the shinbone alley tenement which was once Wright's home: Tough it out, Jack, tough it out.

"With two exceptions," Mencken observed in 1930, "there is not a single novelist deserving the attention of the civilized reader's notice who has not sprung from the Chicago palatinate."

Out of the Twisted Twenties flowered the promise of Chicago as the homeland and heartland of an American renaissance, a place of poets and sculptors to come, of singers and painters, dancers, actors and actresses of golden decades yet to be. Jane Addams and Bix Beiderbecke and Mary Garden and Billy Petrolle and Grover Cleveland Alexander were working their happy wonders then. Gene Field had gone, but Dreiser and Anderson and Masters and Sandburg were still here.

Thirty years later we stand on the rim of a cultural Sahara with not a camel in sight. The springs dried up and the sands drifted in, and the caravans went the other way. The names of our writers are one with the fighters whose names are legends: Battling Nelson and Barney Ross, Willie Joyce and Tony Zale, Tuffy Griffiths and Miltie Aron, Billy Marquart and Davey Day. Today, whether speaking of writers or fighters or ballplayers, the only true major-leaguers batting hereabouts are all working out of Comiskey Park.

(And what became of No-Hit Charley Robertson, who stepped off a sandlot one afternoon to pitch that perfect game for the White Sox? What ever became of No-Hit Charley, who put twenty-seven men down on strikeouts and infield popups—and then stepped back to his sandlot and left nothing behind but that perfect afternoon when nobody in the world could get a hit?)

And what became of the old Bismarck Gardens, that stood where the Marigold stands now? What became of Sam T. Jack's Burlesque and the old Globe on Desplaines? Who remembers the electrified fountain that was once the showpiece of Lincoln Park? Who now knows the sorrowful long-ago name of the proud steamer *Chicora*, down with all hands in the ice off South Haven? Or where all the high-wheeled open-front hacks went, with the velvet robe in the back and the jack handle in front in case of trouble? Gone with the days when Patrick Henry beer sold for four dollars a quarter barrel and White Swan gin for twenty-nine cents a half pint; gone with Emile Coué, gone with old Sam Insull, gone with Billy Sunday, gone with Great Man Shires. Sunk under the ice in the waves off South Haven, sunk with all hands for good and forever, for keeps and a single day.

The city today is more a soldier's than an artist's town. It has had its big chance, and fluffed it. Thirty years ago we gave musicians to the world; now we give drill sergeants and "professional informants," formerly just "informers."

You can live in a natural home, with pictures on the walls, or you can live in a fort; but it's a lead-pipe cinch you can't live in both. You can't make an arsenal of a nation and yet expect its great cities to produce artists. It's in the nature of the overbraided brass to build walls about the minds of men—as it is in the nature of the arts to tear those dark walls down. Today, under the name of "security," the dark shades are being drawn.

Yet, looking east to the cocktail-lounge culture of New York or west to the drawn shades of Hollywood, where directors go on all-fours begging producers, "Please kick me, it will show the world how deeply I respect you," we can agree complacently with the old ward-heeler from Wells and Monroe telling the visiting crusader, "A lot *you* got to holler."

A lot we all got to holler.

"Watch out for yourself" is still the word. "What can I do for you?" still means "What can you do for me?" around these parts—and that's supposed to make this the most American of cities too. It's always been an artist's town and it's always been a torpedo's town, the most artistic characters in the strong-arm industry as well as the world's most muscular poets get that way just by growing up in Chicago—and that's an American sort of arrangement too they tell us.

So whether you're in the local writing racket or in the burglary line, if you're not a bull then you'd better be a fox. Wise up, Jim: it's a joint where the bulls and the foxes live well and the lambs wind up head-down from the hook. On the day that the meek inherit the rest of the earth they'll be lining up here for unemployment insurance and be glad to be getting it.

A town where the artist of class and the swifter-type thief approach their work with the same lofty hope of slipping a fast one over on everybody and making a fast buck to boot. "If he can get away with it I give the man credit," is said here of both bad poets and good safe-blowers. Write, paint or steal the town blind—so long as you make your operation pay off you'll count nothing but dividends and hear nothing but cheers. Terrible Tommy O'Connor was never a hero till he walked past the hangman and out the door and never came back any more.

Make the *Tribune* bestseller list and the Friends of American Writers, the Friends of Literature, the Friends of Shakespeare and the Friends of Frank Harris will be tugging at your elbow, tittering down your collar, coyly sneaking an extra olive into your martini or drooling flatly right into your beer with the drollest sort of flattery and the cheapest grade of praise: the grade reserved strictly for proven winners.

But God help you if you're a loser and unproven to boot: the bushytails will stone your very name. "Hit him again, he don't own a dime" is the rock upon which the Gold Coast literati have builded along with the blowsiest North Clark Street tart. "Let's see your dirty gold, Jack," is how you're judged on either The Coast or The Street. "This is a high-class parlor, we ain't doin' business in no gangway, bud."

Therefore its poets pull the town one way while its tycoons' wives pull it another, its gunmen making it the world's crime capital while its educators beat the bushes for saints. Any old saints. And every time a Robert Hutchins or a Robert Morss Lovett pulls it half an inch out of the mud, a Hearst or an Insull or a McCormick shoves it down again by sheer weight of wealth and venality.

Up, down and lurching sidewise—small wonder we're such a Johnson of a joint. Small wonder we've had trouble growing up.

The very toughest sort of town, they'll tell you—
that's what makes it so American.

Yet it isn't any tougher at heart than the U.S.A. is
tough at heart, for all her ships at sea. It just acts with
the nervous violence of the two-timing bridegroom whose
guilt is more than he can bear: the bird who tries to
throw his bride off the scent by accusing her of infidelity
loudly enough for the neighbors to hear. The guiltier he
feels the louder he talks. That's the sort of little loud
talker we have in Chicago today. He isn't a tough punk,
he's just a scared one. Americans everywhere face gun-
fire better than guilt.

Making this not only the home park of the big soap-
chip and sausage-stuffing tycoons, the home cave of the
juke-box giants and the mail-order dragons, the knot
that binds the TV waves to the airlanes and the railroad
ties to the sea, but also the psychological nerve center
where the pang goes deepest when the whole country
is grinding its teeth in a nightmare sleep.

Here, where we've kept the frontier habit of the Big
Bluff most intact, the hearts of Americans, who must
go along with the Big Bluff or be investigated, are most
troubled.

Congressman Lincoln once told Polk that he was
"like a man on a hot shovel finding no place on which
he could sit down," meaning that the torch Polk's brass
was putting to another people's fields was not Democracy's torch after all. If he could say a word in Springfield
again this morning he might assure us that we've got
the wrong shovel again.

Here, where hope was highest, the disappointment digs deepest.

You can't push nineteen-year-olds who want to be good doctors and good engineers into a war for the salvation of importers' investments and expect them to come out believing in anything much beyond the uses of the super-bazooka against "gooks." You can see the boys who stopped caring in 1917 under the city arc-lamps yet.

Under the tall lamps yet. As evening comes taxiing in and the jungle hiders come softly forth: geeks and gargoyles, old blown winoes, sour stewbums and grinning ginsoaks, young dingbats who went ashore on D Plus One or D Plus Two and have been trying to find some arc-lit shore ever since. Strolling with ancient box-car perverts who fought all their wars on the Santa Fe.

Deserters' faces, wearing the very latest G.I. issue: the plastic masks of an icy-cold despair. Where the sick of heart and the lost in spirit stray. From the forgotten battlegrounds on the other side of the billboards, on the other side of the TV commercials, the other side of the headlines. Fresh from the gathering of snipes behind the nearest KEEP OFF warnings come the forward patrols of tomorrow. Every day is D-day under the El.

By highway and by byway, along old rag-tattered walls, surprised while coming up in the grass by the trolley's green-fire flare, their faces reveal, in that ash-green flash, a guilt never their very own.

Upon the backstreets of some postwar tomorrow, when the city is older yet, these too shall live by night.

Bright faces of tomorrow: whiskey-heads and hopheads, old cokey-joes and musclemen on the prowl for one last wandering square to muscle before the final arc-lamp dims. When the poolrooms all are padlocked and the juke-boxes all are still. When the glasses all are empty. And, under the torn and sagging ties of the long-blasted El, the last survivors cook up the earth's final mulligan. To toast man's earth derisively with the earth's last can of derail: "Let's give it back to the squares."

When traffic no longer picks up, as traffic used to do.

"When it come to Democracy they had to take *our* brand in them days," surviving veterans may recall. "Our brand or else. The goon squads saw to *that*. They went out of business shortly after that." We all went out of business shortly after that.

These are the pavement-colored thousands of the great city's nighttime streets, a separate race with no place to go and the whole long night to kill. And no Good-Morning nor Good-Evening-Dears for the freshly combed tribe of Riders-to-Work-by-Morning nor the dusty-collared clan of Riders-to-Home-by-Dusk.

Tonight, just as the daylight's last sleepy Boy Scout is being tucked in with a kiss and a prayer, the sullen evening's earliest torpedo slips the long cue silently from the shadowy rack. Touches the shaded lamp above the green-baized cloth and turns on the night.

Every day is D-day under the El.

6

No more giants

It used to be a writer's town and it's always been a fighter's town. For writers and fighters and furtive torpedoes, cat-bandits, baggage thieves, hallway head-lockers on the prowl, baby photographers and stylish coneroos, this is the spot that is always most convenient, being so centrally located, for settling ancestral grudges. Whether the power is in a .38, a typewriter ribbon or a pair of six-ouncers, the place has grown great on bone-deep grudges: of writers and fighters and furtive torpedoes.

"City of the big shoulders" was how the white-haired poet put it. Maybe meaning that the shoulders had to get that wide because they had so many bone-deep grudges to settle. The big dark grudge cast by the four standing in white muslin robes, hands cuffed behind, at the gallows' head. For the hope of the eight-hour day.

The grudge between Grover Cleveland and John Peter Altgeld. The long deep grudges still borne for McCormick the Reaper, for Pullman and Pullman's Gary. Grudges like heavy hangovers from men and women whose fathers were not yet born when the bomb was thrown, the court was rigged, and the deed was done.

And maybe it's a poet's town for the same reason it's a working stiff's town, both poet and working stiff being boys out to get even for funny cards dealt by an overpaid houseman weary long years ago.

And maybe it's a working stiff's and a poet's town because it's also an American Legionnaire's town, real Chamber of Commerce territory, the big banker-and-broker's burg, where a softclothes dick with a paunch and no brain at all, simply no brain at all, decides what movies and plays we ought to see and what we mustn't. An arrangement sufficient to make a sensitive burglar as well as a sensitive poet look around for the tools closest to hand.

Town of the hard and bitter strikes and the trigger-happy cops, where any good burglar with a sheet a foot long can buy a pass at a C-note per sheet: half a sheet, half a bill. Two sheets, two bills. Yes, and where the aces will tell the boy behind the bars, "Come on out of there, punk. You ain't doin' us no good in there. Out on the street 'n get it up—everythin' over a C you get to keep for yourself 'n be in court with it at nine tomorrow or we'll pick you up without it 'n fit you for a jacket."

Where undried blood on the pavement and undried blood on the field yet remembers Haymarket and Memorial Day.

Most radical of all American cities: Gene Debs' town, Big Bill Haywood's town, the One-Big-Union town. Where woodworkers once came out on the First of May wearing pine shavings in their caps, brewers followed still wearing their aprons, and behind them the bakers, the barbers, the cornice-makers, tin-roofers and lumber-shovers, trailed by clerks and salesmen. As well as the town where the race riots of 1919 broke and the place where the professional anti-Semites still set up shop confident of a strong play from the North Shore.

Town of the flagpole sitters, iron city, where everything looks so old yet the people look so young. And the girl who breaks the world's record for being frozen into blocks of ice between sprints at the Coliseum Walkathon breaks the selfsame record every night. And of that adolescent who paused in his gum-chewing, upon hearing the sentence of death by electrocution passed upon him, to remember ever so softly: "Knew I'd never get to be twenny-one anyhow."

Town of the small, cheerful apartments, the beer in the icebox, the pipes in the rack, the children well behaved and the TV well tuned, the armchairs fatly upholstered and the record albums filed: 33 rpm, 45 rpm, 78 rpm. Where the 33 rpm husband and proud father eats all his vitamin-stuffed dinner cautiously and then streaks to the bar across the street to drink himself senseless among strangers, at 78 rpm, all alone.

Town of the great international clowns, where the transcontinental Barnum-and-Bailey buffoons stand on their heads for a picture on the sports page, a round of applause, a wardful of votes, a dividend or a friendly smile: Big Bill Thompson, King Levinsky, Yellow Kid Weil, Gorgeous George, Sewell Avery, Elizabeth Dilling, Joe Beauharnais, Sam Insull, Botsy Connors, Shipwreck Kelly, The Great I Am, and Oliver J. Dragon. And, of course, the Only-One-on-Earth, the inventor of modern warfare, our very own dime-store Napoleon, Colonel McGooseneck.

Town of the classic boners and the All-Time All-American bums, where they score ten runs after two are gone in the last of the ninth when the left-fielder drops an easy popup that should have been the third out. Final score: 10–8. Where somebody is always forgetting to touch second. And the local invincible, the boy most likely to be champion, faints open-eyed on the ropes in the very first round without being struck a blow because the champion is coming right toward him.

"I'll do any damned thing you boys want me to do," Mayor Kelly told his boys gratefully, and he kept his word.

Town of the great Lincolnian liberals, the ones who stuck out their stubborn necks in the ceaseless battle between the rights of Owners and the rights of Man, the stiff-necked wonders who could be broken but couldn't be bent: Dreiser, Altgeld, Debs.

The only town for certain where a Philadelphia first-baseman can answer an attractive brunette's invitation to step into her room: "I have a surprise for you"—and meet a shotgun blast under the heart. "The urge kept nagging at me and the tension built up. I thought killing someone would relieve it." For the sad heart's long remembrance.

Town of the blind and crippled newsies and the pinboys whose eyes you never see at all. Of the Montgomery-Ward sleepwalkers and all the careworn hopers from home with Expressman Death in their eyes reading all about it on the Garfield Park Local.

Town of the topless department stores, floor upon floor upon floor, where a sea-green light from the thousand-globed chandeliers drifts down the scented air, across oriental rugs and along long gleaming glass: where wait the fresh-cut sirloin tips, the great bloody T-bones and the choice center-cut pork chops, all with a freezing disdain for the ground hamburger.

A Jekyll-and-Hyde sort of burg, where one university's faculty members can protest sincerely against restrictive covenants on the blighted streets bordering their campus—not knowing that the local pay roll draws on real estate covered by covenants like a tent. Let's get back to them saints, Professor. It's awful cold out there.

As the carillons of twelve A.M. divide the campus from the slum.

"The slums take their revenge," the white-haired poet warned us thirty-two American League seasons and Lord-Knows-How-Many-Swindles-Ago. "Always somehow or other their retribution can be figured in any community."

The slums take their revenge. And you can take your pick of the avengers among the fast international set at any district-station lockup on any Saturday night. The lockups are always open and there are always new faces. Always someone you never met before, and where they all come from nobody knows and where they'll go from here nobody cares.

The giants cannot come again; all the bright faces of tomorrow are careworn hustlers' faces.

And the place always gets this look of some careworn hustler's tomorrow by night, as the arch of spring is mounted and May turns into June. It is then that the women come out of the summer hotels to sit one stone step above the pavement, surveying the men curb-sitting one step below it. Between them pass the nobodies from nowhere, the nobodies nobody knows, with faces cut from the same cloth as their caps, and the women whose eyes reflect nothing but the pavement.

The nameless, useless nobodies who sleep behind the taverns, who sleep beneath the El. Who sleep in burnt-out busses with the windows freshly curtained;

in winterized chicken coops or patched-up truck bodies. The useless, helpless nobodies nobody knows: that go as the snow goes, where the wind blows, there and there and there, down any old cat-and-ashcan alley at all. There, unloved and lost forever, lost and unloved for keeps and a day, there far below the ceaseless flow of TV waves and FM waves, way way down there where no one has yet heard of phonevision nor considered the wonders of technicolor video—there, there below the miles and miles of high-tension wires servicing the miles and miles of low-pressure cookers, there, there where they sleep on someone else's pool table, in someone else's hall or someone else's jail, there where they chop kindling for heat, cook over coal stoves, still burn kerosene for light, there where they sleep the all-night movies through and wait for rain or peace or snow: there, there beats Chicago's heart.

There, unheard by the millions who ride the waves above and sleep, and sleep and dream, night after night after night, loving and well beloved, guarding and well guarded, beats the great city's troubled heart.

And all the stately halls of science, the newest Broadway hit, the endowed museums, the endowed opera, the endowed art galleries, are not for their cold pavement-colored eyes. For the masses who do the city's labor also keep the city's heart. And they think there's something fishy about someone giving them a museum for nothing and free admission on Saturday afternoons.

They sense somebody got a bargain, and they are so right. The city's arts are built upon the uneasy consciences that milked the city of millions on the grain exchange, in traction and utilities and sausage-stuffing and then bought conscience-ease with a minute fraction of the profits. A museum for a traction system, an opera building for a utilities empire. Therefore the arts themselves here, like the acres of Lorado Taft's deadly handiwork, are largely statuary. Mere monuments to the luckier brokers of the past. So the people shy away from their gifts, they're never sure quite why.

The place remains a broker's portage. And an old-time way station for pimps as well. Both professions requiring the same essential hope of something for nothing and a soft-as-goosefeathers way to go. A portage too for the fabulous engines: the Harvester, the sleeping car and the Bessemer Process.

Yet never a harvest in sight hereabouts for humanity's spirit, uprooted over half the world and well deceived here at home.

No room, no time, no breath for the Bessemer processes of the heart.

7

Nobody knows where O'Connor went

An October sort of city even in spring. With somebody's washing always whipping, in smoky October colors off the third-floor rear by that same wind that drives the yellowing comic strips down all the gutters that lead away from home. A hoarse-voiced extry-hawking newsie of a city.

By its padlocked poolrooms and its nightshade neon, by its carbarn Christs punching transfers all night long; by its nuns studying gin-fizz ads in the Englewood Local, you shall know Chicago.

By nights when the yellow salamanders of the El bend all one way and the cold rain runs with the red-lit rain. By the way the city's million wires are burdened only by lightest snow; and the old year yet lighter upon them. When chairs are stacked and glasses are turned and arc-lamps all are dimmed. By days when the wind bangs alley gates ajar and the sun goes by on the wind. By nights when the moon is an only child above the measured thunder of the cars, you may know Chicago's heart at last:

You'll know it's the place built out of Man's ceaseless failure to overcome himself. Out of Man's endless war against himself we build our successes as well as our failures. Making it the city of all cities most like Man himself—loneliest creation of all this very old poor earth.

And Shoeless Joe, who lost his honor and his job, is remembered now more fondly here, when stands are packed and a striped sun burns across them, than old Comiskey, who salvaged his own.

On hot and magic afternoons when only the press box, high overhead, divides the hustler and the square.

For there's a left-hander's wind moving down Thirty-fifth, rolling the summer's last straw kelly across second into center, where fell the winning single of the first winning Comiskey team in thirty-two seasons.

Thirty-two American League seasons (and Lord knows how many swindles ago), Nephew is doing thirty-days again for the fifteenth or the thirty-ninth time (this time for defacing private property), nobody knows were O'Connor went and a thousand Happy-Days-Are-Here-Again tunes have come and gone. And the one that keeps coming back softest of all, when tavern lights come on and the night is impaled by the high-tension wires, goes:

> It's only a paper moon
> Hanging over a cardboard sea

For everybody takes care of himself under this paper moon, and the hustlers still handle the cardboard. Joe Felso doesn't trouble his pointy little head just because somebody tossed a rock through some other Joe Felso's window two doors down. It wasn't his window and it wasn't his rock and we all have our own troubles, Jack.

The big town is getting something of Uncle Johnson's fixed look, like that of a fighter working beyond his strength and knowing it. "Laughing even as an ignorant fighter laughs, who has never lost a battle," the white-haired Poet wrote before his hair turned white.

But the quality of our laughter has altered since that appraisal, to be replaced by something sounding more like a juke-box running down in a deserted bar. Chicago's laughter has grown metallic, the city no longer laughs easily and well, out of spiritual good health. We seem to have no way of judging either the laughter of the living or the fixed smirk of the dead.

The slums take their revenge. How much did he *have*, is what we demand to know when we hear good old Joe Felso has gone to his reward. Never what *was* he, in human terms. Was his income listed publicly? Was there a Ford in his future at the very moment he was snatched? And whether he was of any use or any joy to himself, when he had his chance for use and joy, we never seem to wonder. It's hustle and bustle from day to day, chicken one day and feathers the next, and nobody knows where O'Connor went.

Nobody will tell how Tommy got free.

Nor whether there are well-springs here for men beneath the rubble of last year's revelry.

The pig-wallows are paved, great Diesels stroke noiselessly past the clamorous tenements of home. The Constellations move, silently and all unseen, through blowing seas above the roofs. Only the measured clatter of the empty cars, where pass the northbound and the southbound Els, comes curving down the constant boundaries of night.

The cemetery that yet keeps the Confederate dead is bounded by the same tracks that run past Stephen A. Douglas' remains. The jail where Parsons hung is gone, and the building from which Bonfield marched is no more. Nobody remembers the Globe on Desplaines, and only a lonely shaft remembers the four who died, no one ever understood fully why. And those who went down with the proud steamer *Chicora* are one with those who went down on the *Eastland*. And those who sang "My God, How the Money Rolls In" are one with those who sang, "Brother, Can You Spare a Dime?"

And never once, on any midnight whatsoever, will you take off from here without a pang. Without forever feeling something priceless is being left behind in the forest of furnished rooms, lost forever down below, beneath the miles and miles of lights and lights. With the slow smoke blowing compassionately across them like smoke across the spectrum of the heart. As smoky rainbows dreaming, and fading as they dream, across those big fancy Southside jukes forever inviting you to put another nickel in, put another nickel in whether the music is playing or not.

As the afternoon's earliest juke-box beats out rumors of the Bronzeville night.

A rumor of neon flowers, bleeding all night long, along those tracks where endless locals pass.

Leaving us empty-handed every hour on the hour.

Remembering nights, when the moon was a buffalo moon, that the narrow plains between the billboards were touched by an Indian wind. Littered with tin cans and dark with smoldering rubble, an Indian wind yet finds, between the shadowed canyons of The Loop, patches of prairie to touch and pass.

Between the curved steel of the El and the nearest Clark Street hockshop, between the penny arcade and the shooting gallery, between the basement ginmill and the biggest juke in Bronzeville, the prairie is caught for keeps at last. Yet on nights when the blood-red neon of the tavern legends tether the arc-lamps to all the puddles left from last night's rain, somewhere between the bright carnival of the boulevards and the dark girders of the El, ever so far and ever so faintly between the still grasses and the moving waters, clear as a cat's cry on a midnight wind, the Pottawattomies mourn in the river reeds once more.

The Pottawattomies were much too square. They left nothing behind but their dirty river.

While we shall leave, for remembrance, one rusty iron heart.

The city's rusty heart, that holds both the hustler and the square.

Takes them both and holds them there.

For keeps and a single day.

Afterword

THE PEOPLE OF THESE PARTS:

A survey of modern Mid-American letters

"The people of these parts address each other as Mulai (Lord) and Sayyid (Sir), and use the expressions 'Your servant' and 'Your Excellency'. When one meets another, instead of giving the ordinary greeting, he says respectfully, 'Here is your slave' or 'Here is your servant at your service'. These make presents of honorifics to each other. Gravity with them is a fabulous affair."

Notes on the condition of the city of Damascus from the tenth of August to the eighth of September in the year 1184, from a chronicle of the Spanish Moor Abu-1 —Husayn Muhammed ibn Ahmad ibn Jubayr.

I. "What is literature?" Jean-Paul Sartre once asked in a small volume bearing that title.

I submit that literature is made upon any occasion that a challenge is put to the legal apparatus by conscience in touch with humanity.

Now we all know.

When the city clerk of Terre Haute refused to issue warrents for arrest of streetwalkers in spite of his sworn legal duty to issue warrants for arrest of streetwalkers, and instead demanded of the Terre Haute police, "Why don't you make war on people in high life instead of upon these penniless girls?" the little sport performed an act of literature.

"These men were put to death because they made you nervous," an American poet summed up the case of Massachusetts vs. Sacco and Vanzetti better than the judge.

We are a people with too many nervous judges.

"Had I so interfered in behalf of any of that class, every man in the court would have deemed it an act worthy of reward rather than punishment," John Brown explained his own assault upon a legal apparatus gone out of touch with humanity.

Old Brown of Osawatomie didn't know that nobody was going to give him a banquet for pulling the judge off the bench down into the dock.

"I repeat that I am the enemy of the 'order' of today and I repeat that I shall combat it. I despise your order, your laws, your force-propped authority. Hang me for it!" was how a twenty-year-old once went to his death for practicing reckless politics in Chicago.

The history of American letters, in this strict view, is a record of apparently senseless assaults upon standard operating procedure, commonly by a single driven man. Followed, after the first shock of surprise, (conscience in any courtroom always coming as a surprise) by a counter-assault mounted by a judge using a gavel as a blackjack, a court-stenographer armed with a fingernail file and an editorialist equally intent on getting in a bit of gouging before cocktail time: each enthusiastically assisted by cops wielding pistol-butts and clergymen swinging two-by-fours nailed in the shape of crosses.

In less time than it takes to say "Emile Zola" everyone is standing around congratulating one another for having protected society, because if the stiff wasn't guilty of something why was the stiff bleeding so hard? He must of been some kind of nut.

And the old earth sighs *heigh-o, the wind and the rain,* having made this scene before.

Ultimately it develops that Some-Kind-of-Nut was the only party in court in his right mind. Whereupon everyone reveals that he was secretly on Some-Kind-Of-Nut's side all along, especially the editorialist.

And the earth takes a few more heigh-ho spins.

Having made this scene before.

The hard necessity of bringing the judge on the bench down into the dock has been the peculiar responsibility of the writer in all ages of man. In Chicago, in our own curious span, we have seesawed between blind assault and blind counter-assault, hanging men in one decade for beliefs which, in another, we honor others.

And that there has hardly been an American writer of stature who has not come up through The Chicago Palatinate, was an observation which, when somebody first made it, was still true. God help the poor joker who comes up through Old Seesaw Chicago today.

For we are now in a gavel-and-fingernail era. Punitive cats have the upper hand. The struggle is not to bring the judge into the dock, but to see who can get closest to him on the bench. For upon the bench is where the power is, and elbows are flying. Between TV poseurs, key-club operators and retarded Kilgallens in charge of columns, any writer whose thought is simply to report the sights and sounds of the city must be some kind of nut.

And let the word get around that Some-Kind-of-Nut has been taking films of the ordinary streets of day, rather than of interiors of salons not one Chicagoan in ten thousand ever sees, and some fantasist from Balaban & Katz will put it down sight unseen—"*Art?*" he asks, and answers himself, "art is nuts." Another thinker will then produce an editorial protesting that "it represents an imbalanced picture of the city"—(the one phrase required to be a Chicago editorial writer)—and the mayor, an old-shoe guy who hasn't seen it either, will promptly have it banned by a board of redcaps because "it would not serve the public interest," in a city whose pleasures are so chaste as those of Chicago.

"What do you want? A bloody travelog?" one of Europe's top film-makers asked when informed that the documentary he had made of Chicago could not be shown because art is nuts.

But a bloody travelog is, of course, precisely what is wanted. Because that's how things are in the sodden old Palatinate these days, men. That's what it's really like in Chicago this morning.

There are a number of answers to the old query about why writers so often take a one-way flight from Midway or O'Hare and never come back here. One answer becomes self-evident to anyone who has witnessed a henyard full of hipless biddies entitling themselves "Friends of Literature" in the act of honoring Shakespeare and Lincoln. It looks more like they had Frank Harris in mind but I'm sure they don't eat that way at home. Another reason is that the medieval nonentities of City Hall who have gotten the work of Rossellini, Sartre and Denis Mitchell outlawed here don't care for the local talent either. Any bookkeeper speaking in the name of Balaban & Katz Forever can make it plain enough that the town isn't all it's cracked up to be in *Town and Country*.

San Francisco has more daring. For there, even though their men write like boys, there are listeners who are ready to hear somebody speak in a voice that is new, saying something not said before, who will be better than anybody up till now.

Yet Chicago is the same city in which a literature bred by hard times on the river, hard times on the range and hard times in the town once became a world literature.

It's the same town that once carried a literature emanating from large feelings to all men in all tongues.

For it was here that those arrangements more convenient to owners of property than to the propertyless were most persistently contested by the American conscience.

Chicago has progressed, culturally, from being The Second City to being The Second-Hand City. The vital cog in our culture now is not the artist, but the middleman whose commercial status lends art the aura of status when he acquires a collection of originals. The word "culture" now means nothing more than "approved." It isn't what is exhibited so much that matters as where: that being where one meets the people who matter.

Of concern for the great city's night-colors, its special sounds like those of no other city, for its ceaseless dramas lived out behind blind doors; or for the jargon-tongue of Chicagoese as spoken in our Saturday night dance-halls, bars and bookies and courts, there is less than approval. The *Dziennik Chicagoski* will get you if you don't watch out. The Polish Roman Catholic Union, having recently purchased Milwaukee Avenue, wants its property boosted, not described. Any report on the local scene that cuts truthfully is like pitching a house-brick through a window of *The Polish Daily Zgoda*— the ladies will be at the Chicago Public Library in no time at all getting you off the shelves—not a difficult job at all. No, the life of a free-lance journalist is not a happy one.

Yesterday's Paris is more real by remembrance than today's Chicago. Paris in the afternoon is part of all the city's afternoons; but afternoon in Chicago is just another day.

For Chicago lives like a drunken El-rider who cannot remember where he got on nor at what station he wants to get off. The sound of wheels moving below satisfies him that he is making great progress.

Yet now, after the wheels have turned without cease for a hundred years, compare the faces of a family group of Europeans, first-generation Chicagoans of five decades ago, with the faces standing in line to get into a Loop theatre today; and you see too many faces that have lost responsibility even toward themselves.

These are the faces of occupying troops, and occupying troops make false lovers. So there is a truth told by a fool, one Colonel Jack Reilly, speaking for the mayor, explaining why Denis Mitchell's BBC documentary was banned here: "People in Chicago don't know about these things, so why bother them?"

Thus the Chicago of the nineteen-forties is unrecorded and that of the fifties is sunk for keeps. A thousand dollars' worth of film and sound equipment could salvage remembrance of a time that will not come again. But the colonel is right—we hear the heroic thunder of a million wheels below—why bother whether we race against time uphill or down, so long as the race goes on?

Which explains, in part, the paradox that Europeans are more concerned about the city than ourselves. A paradox that makes a heartening discovery for a Chicago writer whose books are not available in the Chicago public library, to find them available in every large city of Europe.

The writer, of course, is always an egotist who wants to see his name on everything he writes, whether it is good or bad. The editorialist is less inclined to expose his personality to the public eye. He prefers anonymity.

"A Case For Ra(n)t Control" was the clever caption of the editorial with which *The Chicago Daily News* greeted the present essay, followed by a serious demand for "revocation of the author's poetic license"; whatever that may mean.

Mediocrity is never a passive lack of originality: it avenges its deprivation. Affording it anonymity, like furnishing a toothless man with artificial teeth, excites it toward taking measures. It wishes to bite something that will not bite back.

Between the majestic drumroll of the great *Daily News* presses, like the roll of infallibility itself, one may hear, by listening closely, a tiny intermittent clicking of false teeth.

"A more partial, distorted, unenviable slant was never taken by a man pretending to cover the Chicago story—a book unlikely to please anyone but masochists—definitely a highly-scented object," a busy little object who didn't smell too sweet himself typed busily away at *The Tribune:* the job of assistant travel editor was open.

Now, a decade late, it would appear that a heavy infiltration of masochists from abroad has succeeded in gaining permanency for the book.

And what of our busy typist, dear reader? Did he make assistant travel editor? Will success spoil him? Has he found a master who doesn't mind that he has never been housebroken?

The truth is that, in order to misrepresent an author, it is not necessary for a book-reviewer to quote him out of context. He needs only to impose the established tone of his paper upon that in which the book is written. The tone of "there shall be no difference between them and the rest" may thus be reduced to meaning that all men should dress, speak and think alike.

This journalistic gypsy-switch, this trick of substituting counterfeit values for true ones, leaves few readers, of the multitudes who read the *Tribune*'s Sunday book-review, aware that they are really reading, not book-reviews, but editorials.

Nor is the gypsy-switch, as used by the *Tribune*, limited to that paper. It is the tone that now dominates Chicago in the arts as well as politics. Mediocrity is wanted. Mediocrity is solicited. Mediocrity is honored. And mediocrity will not put up with originality.

To the professional mediocrity, therefore, Chicago is today a city of golden opportunity; whether he reviews books on television or for the *Tribune*. But to the writer seeking to work creatively, it is a kick in the palatinate.

When Whitman wrote that "there shall be no difference between them and the rest" he made the great American beginning for a literature expressing an exuberant good humor: which yet sought darkly for understanding of Man.

Now the new word rides proudly traffic-borne on the sides of newspaper trucks racing from newsstand to newsstand assuring us of some vast difference between us and the rest; because the rest are sleeping with women all over the Southside and the police are denying everything.

"The more we put into welfare the worse the immorality becomes," one columnist advances the concept that immorality on the Southside derives from accepting public welfare. In which event we better start tailing a few people in Glenview who have two cars as they must be on welfare too.

"They're multiplying like guinea pigs out there," this immaculately-conceived Hildy Johnson warns us— "We are making it profitable to have babies out of wedlock! The soaring rate of illegitimacies shows that the more help you give, the more indolent the recipient becomes! Where will the vicious cycle of bastardy end?"

Then leaves the office early because his wife is having friends in for cocktails and you never can tell when an unattached chick might turn up.

When the present essay appeared, the curtain was already dropping on the larger point of view. It was written out of awareness that multitudes live among us who share the horrors but not the marvels of our split-level Bedlam. As well as from a natural resentment toward a press whose complacency could not be dented. For no man can make a dent in emptiness.

"We have had a feeling which has persisted for sometime," a *Chicago Sun-Times* hand recently tried to place a persistent feeling, "that squalor is going out of fashion in Chicago. Perhaps this is largely due to the postwar war on slums, our mayor's efforts in tidying up the streets, the popularity of cheering colors and the wide interest in art and music shown by the public.

"All these, and more, have added up to a feeling that the good old-fashioned, smelly squalor immortalized by men of literary genius is definitely on the way out.

"To strengthen that sense comes along the Schenley advertising display of modern masterpieces in the subway . . . dispelling the sordid gloom of our subway decor, and adds a touch of brightness to the day for the weary homeward bound."

It depends upon which way you're homeward-bound, Weary.

Actually, Mr. Weary doesn't give a tinker's damn how bleak any street is, so long as it isn't the one on which *he* drives home.

Recent protests, following disclosure that policemen were using squadrols to steal electric kitchen appliances, were really cries of outrage at the officers' highhanded dismissal of the professional burglar who has served the department loyally. This is a service city, and when you use your own car and do the driving yourself you put another man out of work. In this instance it was the professional burglar who was given notice; but every other middleman in town felt apprehensive. Public indignation toward the police was provoked because, on top of everything else, the department had been sloppy. It wasn't Tony Accardo, but James C. Hagerty, who advised us all: "Don't get caught."

One Richard Morrison, a youth already in trouble for stealing change out of a *Tribune* box on Lake Shore Drive, brought the original charges against the officers. One judge immediately quashed burglary and conspiracy charges against eight policemen and a second judge discovered an indictment against two detectives to be useless because the state had used a comma instead of a semi-colon.

When informed by a third judge that he was being held illegally and was free to leave the court, young Morrison held fast to the safety of the witness chair. He had been semi-coloned into being a moving target and he knew it.

"The way I feel now," he told reporters, "is that if what I did doesn't help, this city will never be cleaned up. When I get out, I'll always be looking over my shoulder, even if I can go straight as I want to do. There'll always be people who will want to look me up."

They will, son, they will. They did. And when you wind up in the alley with the cats looking at you, that will be one more step in dispelling the sordid gloom of our subway decor.

To add a touch of brightness to the day for the weary homeward bound.

II. If America's Richard Morrisons have gained the concern of her novelists, so have her novelists gained stature by concern for America's losers.

The search for the great white whale by the foredoomed hero Ahab, across dangerous seas, was extended, across the deeps of the American conscience, by Dreiser's equally foredoomed youth, Clyde Griffiths, pursuing Success.

Emerging into a ripjaw-and-tearclaw civilization disguised by signs reading, "If-You-Can't-Stop-Smile-As-You-Pass-By," he tried smiling his defenselessness away by assuring his superiors, "Yes Sir, I will do just as you say, Sir. Yes Sir, I understand, Sir." until he had smiled his way into a court-room on trial for his life, listening to a prosecuting attorney describing one Clyde Griffiths:

"Seduction! Seduction! The secret and intended and immoral and illegal and socially unwarranted use of her body outside the regenerative ennobling pale of matrimony! *That* was his purpose, gentlemen!"

It was then too late for the youth to learn that the images along the chamber of mirages were false. That the signs saying, Smile-Darn-You-Smile, camouflaged a struggle for survival as ferocious as that between bulldogs in a bulldog-pit.

Yes Sir. I understand Sir, I will do just as you say, Sir.

"I didn't know I was alive until I killed," another

candidate to the company of men, one who also walked through mirages but finally made it the hard way, explains himself in the final chapter of Wright's *Native Son*. But Bigger Thomas was one who smashed mirrors rather than accept his reflection in them. "It's alright now," is his last word.

Although pictured by the prosecution as men on the hunt, each was himself the prey. Dreiser's method of challenging the legal apparatus and Wright's method were different, but the purpose of both was to demand that those economically empowered disprove their complicity in the crimes for which Clyde Griffiths and Bigger Thomas stood accused. Both writers demanded that the prosecuting attorney show his hands.

The outcast Ahab's pursuit of the great white whale was followed by other strange heroes and heroines more alive in their fictional lives than men and women of real life, and yet—like Ahab—all foredoomed. The search went down Main Street in Winesburg, Ohio, and down Main Street to the edge of town, to where the town's last gas-lamp makes fence and wagon-road look haggard. And on either hand, in town or out, in the General Store or on backland farms, faces of men and women living without alternatives were revealed.

A search past 3 A.M. gas-stations and darkened farms under a moon that said Repose, Repose. Past field and suburb, to where the arc-lamps of Chicago begin; down streets Jennie Gerhardt knew. And everywhere, awake or sleeping, revealing men and women trapped without repose.

This was the sleepless city Dreiser and Sherwood

Anderson found; that Farrell was born in; that Richard Wright came to because he had no other place to go.

Today the arc-lamps light a city whose backstreets are more dangerous than a backtrack of the Kalahari Desert: every three A.M. corner looks hired.

Where a street-corner nineteen-year-old once replied to a judge who had just handed down a verdict of death in the electric chair, "I knew I'd never get to be twenty-one anyhow"—and snapped his bubble-gum.

A novel written around the same bubble-gum snapper, in the early nineteen-forties by the present writer, sustained the anti-legalistic tradition toward society which had distinguished Chicago writers since the early years of the century.

Another novel, told more forcefully at the close of that decade, was lost to this tradition through a presentation which confused it, in the public mind, with a cheap biography of Frank Sinatra.

Yet the spirit of, "I belong to these convicts and prostitutes myself," from which these novels derived, was offered to a reader who was no longer around.

That reader and that spirit have been overwhelmed by the newly affluent cat asking querulously, "What are they doing to me?" because he has just charged off ten thousand dollars in entertainment of friends to the government and is having trouble making it stick. What this new reader wants is not to feel there shall be no difference between him and the rest; but that the difference between himself and the rest be officially recognized by the federal government.

Whitman's offer, bred by hard times on the Middle

Border—"If you tire, give me both burdens"—holds no interest for the boy who has come unburdened into his own the day his Daddy has his name painted beside his own on the front-glass office door. To say "Each man's death diminishes me" today only rouses the alarm of "They're multiplying like guinea pigs out there!"

Well, we're all born equal and anyone in Chicago can now become an expatriate without leaving town.

For there is no room left for the serious writer to stand up in old seesaw Yahoo Chicago.

This is The Middle City, the place where the individual American conscience and formalized opinion has found its sharpest division. The American spirit has discovered its manliest voices, as well as its meanest, here.

At its manliest: Gene Debs saying "While there is a soul in prison I am not free."

At its meanest: see the editorial page of the *Chicago Tribune* any morning of the week. Better yet, take a fast glance at the front page cartoon and walk away: you've just saved seven cents.

Town and Country tells us that "anyone who knows Chicago today will admit it is a beautiful place to live." Now it isn't too difficult for an editor in New York to put a man on a plane to O'Hare Field and helicopter him onto Michigan Boulevard long enough to take a snapshot of a chewing-gum heir stuck up against the side of Papa's building and distribute the tasteless wad in juicy-fruit color as a "Chicago" edition—but *Town and Country* is putting us on. Anyone who lives inside Chicago today has to admit it is a grey subcivilization surrounded by green suburbs.

Or are these loveless castaways watching Clark Kent battling forces of evil in the shadowed lobby of the stag hotel merely awaiting the wave of the future the easy way?

Otherwise, what did that fifteen-year-old mean when he answered the judge who had asked him what he did all day. "I just find a hallway 'n take a shot 'n lean. Just lean 'n dream"?

And what did another teen-ager mean when he told the arresting officers, "Put me in the electric chair, my mother can watch me burn"?

From the bleak inhumanity of our forests of furnished rooms, stretching doorway after anonymous doorway block after block, guarding stairways leading only to numbered doors, from hallways shadowed by fixtures of another day, emerge the dangerous three A.M. boys. Who are not professional burglars nor professional car-thieves nor pete-men nor mobsters (who never fly blind), but are rather those who go on the prowl without themselves knowing what they're after. Their needs criss-cross and they're on the hawks, and will take whatever comes along first—a woman, money, or, just icy pleasure of kicking a queer's teeth down his neck. Whatever wants to happen let the damn thing happen and we'll all read about it in the papers tomorrow. What have *we* got to lose? Say the dangerous boys.

Recalling, ten years later, the outrage expressed by *The Chicago Tribune* and *The Chicago Daily News* at the assertations of this essay, one cannot help but wonder what the reaction might have been had the book cut in closer to what the lives of multitudes are really like on the city's South and West sides. This book didn't begin to tell that story a decade ago; and the story is fully as terrible today as then.

Yet the essay's truths that now seem quaint are drawn from the same wellspring from which Dreiser, Farrell and Wright drew earlier. It still speaks of a hopeful past, of a time that came on too fast; out of a greater concern for the people living in the city than in its transportation problems.

Town and Country's recent congratulations to us for having "an old-shoe guy" for mayor, (one of the best kinds that there are) because he has been known to walk to the corner drug store and bring back an armful of milk shakes for his family, instead of having a detail from Central Police deliver them, seem almost too good to be true. Yet watching the ceaseless all-night traffic moving without a stoplight down the proud new perfect thruway to O'Hare, headlight pursuing tail-light, tail-light fleeing headlight, it is as if each dark unseen driver were not driving, but were driven.

So the city itself moves across the thruway of the years, a city in both flight and pursuit; and surely more driven than driving.

Love is by remembrance. Unlike the people of Paris or London or New York or San Francisco, who prove their love by recording their times in painting and plays and books and films and poetry, the lack of love of Chicagoans for Chicago stands self-evident by the fact that we make no living record of it here. And are, in fact, opposed to first-hand creativity. All we have today of the past is the poetry of Sandburg; now as remote from the Chicago of today as Wordsworth's.

"Late at night, and alone, I am touched by apprehension that we no longer live in America, that we no longer love her. We merely occupy her," Dalton Trumbo writes; reflecting a disconnection, on a national scale, that has transpired here locally.

The most striking development in Chicago since this essay first appeared is neither the construction of The Prudential Building over the I. C. tracks, nor of the Northwest Expressway; but of a change of heart.

For at the very moment when a national effort is being made to extend the great American beginning— that "not one shall be slighted"—to grass huts of the Congo, Hoovervilles of Caracas and to the terribly deprived peoples of India, our local press is passionately preoccupied with the pursuit of barroom drudges sitting in front of whiskey glasses with false bottoms, poor girls trying for their rent money from week to week; or with a woman drawing state aid in support of an illegitimate child who has been entrapped drinking a beer—the mother, not the child.

The presumption that immorality derives largely from acceptance of welfare assistance is a Hearstian concept. So that, although there are no Hearst-owned papers here, whatever paper you buy you still read Hearst.

It strikes me that to disregard human dignity in the interests of circulation makes it more appropriate to regard the men who run the Chicago newspapers as auditors rather than editors. Of what newspaper owner here cannot the same thing be said as the American poet once said of a judge of the Supreme Court of Massachusetts—"these people made you nervous."

Nor can I see in what fashion depriving a woman of her personal dignity, no matter how demeaning her trade, can be justified. If an Eichmann is to be held responsible for lacking a conscience, is not a newspaper owner to be held responsible for employing a columnist who has parlayed an urge to punish into a press pass?

That entrapment, as practiced by at least one columnist here, is illegal even when used by the police department is not the point. The point is that construction of a thruway running without a stoplight from state to state doesn't make any city "a beautiful place to live in" so long as no restraint is put on men armed by the power of the press to hunt down anybody, if such a hunt will help circulation.

And should you say such a woman cannot go unpunished, I must ask in what fashion has she harmed anyone? She has assaulted nobody, robbed nobody, done nothing criminal; yet her chance of staying out of jail is nowhere near as good as that of an electrical utility executive who has made a fortune by price-fixing. Still, everyone feels entitled to punish her.

She does not send for men: they seek her out. And the simple irrefutable fact is that she has been essential to every society, has outlasted every society, is essential to our own and will outlast our own.

So long as the institution of marriage exists she remains essential; for she is not supported by single men, but by married ones.

"Prostitutes everywhere report that their trade is in large measure financed by married men who are weary of the indifference or antagonism of their wives and turn to public women for gratification," Houghton Hooker reports in *Laws of Sex*.

Another thing I intend asking mother about is

whether the papers aren't leaving something out. Every time a girl is made in a raid we get a full description of her: name, age, address and place of employment. What I can't figure out is what was she doing in that room that was so awful if there wasn't somebody just as awful helping her to do something just as awful? If there was a pair of pants on the bed-post, where is the spendthrift who walked into the room inside of them? Are you sure we're not discriminating here? Why isn't *he* entitled to get his name in the paper and a ride downtown? Why don't somebody give *him* a chance to stand up in front of a judge and get fined a hundred dollars or fifty days in County? If everybody is born free and equal as they say, when does *he* get a chance to go to the Chicago Intensive Treatment Hospital for a free checkup? If this is a true democracy, why doesn't he have the same right as any other second-class citizen? It looks like a business-man don't stand a chance in this country any more.

> *"I've seen the people who keep the shops*
> *Merchant or lawyer, whatever you got*
> *And I wouldn't swap you the lowliest wench*
> *For the most high thief on the most high bench*
> *Merchant or lawyer, whatever you got—*
> *God send them mercy—*
> *Then cop the whole lot."*

Crusades from pulpit, court of column against prostitution can have no effect except to divert it to another part of town or from brothel to escort-service, because the basic cause isn't with the women who practice it, but in our own concept of sex. The conviction that sex is basically evil is a perversion out of which prostitution develops. So long as we remain punitive toward sex we are going to have crimes of sex. Indeed, until we recognize sex as a natural urge, pleasant, beautiful, interesting and useful, to be treated, like any other important faculty, such as work or learning, by welcoming it, enjoying it without reverence and permitting discussion of it to be as open as that about art or play or science, we will remain as darkly closeted inside our free-world closet as were the men and women of Salem, Massachusetts, in 1692.

As for the kind of man who conducts the pursuit of the prostitute, that Salem is his trade seems self-evident.

> "Why dost thou lash that whore?
> Strip thine own back
> Thou hotly lust'st to use her in that kind
> For which thou whips't her."

III. Sandburg's Chicago, Dreiser's Chicago, Farrell's and Wright's and my own Chicago, that was somebody else's Chicago. At the time that *Chicago: City on the Make* was published, the curtain was already dropping on that Chicago.

When the curtain went up, it was on a different scene.

Here was a play with a different plot.

Act I: Scene One—Annual Meeting of The Chicago Greater Hollerers Association.

On stage: Chicago's leaders as selected by *Town and Country*.

Sitting in an aisle seat, seeing on stage my city's

suntanned elders just back from the Fontainebleau with their armpits tanned from long days under the rye bread trees, I too applauded the brave flash of their costume jewelry and their high credit ratings.

Yet I felt a pang of secret regret that I had played the black market in soap and cigarettes in Marseille instead of staying home and playing it in automobiles in Detroit and waiting until the war was over to volunteer for overseas duty. For I realized now that one must begin young to become a leader of one's city in middle age.

O, I thought, if there's *really* a little somebody for every boy in the world, why doesn't some little somebody phone *me* and ask, in a voice ever-so-refined, if *I* would conduct a purple-heart cruise for my city? For I too wish to stand at the helm of a water-borne scow to cry "*Now, Voyager!*" while peeling Eskimo pies for handless vets. (I'll peel anything to get a fringe benefit.)

And if I can't earn a fringe benefit myself, won't somebody let me be somebody else's little fringe benefit? Won't somebody send *me* a ten-year-old epileptic to froth for me on a TV marathon? Can't I get to froth on somebody else's marathon for myself? Why won't *anybody* let me find prizes in crackerjack boxes for retarded kids? Is somebody in City Hall afraid I'll steal the prizes? The only prize I want is a deduction for entertaining stupid brats—or am I asking too much? Men, all I want is to tie little Fourth-of-July flags in the wheels of paraplegics' chairs. I'll tie, I'll peel, I'll froth, I'll wheel, I'll lope and double-back, but how am *I* ever to be an old-shoe guy who goes down to the drug store and brings back milk shakes for his family when nobody will let me get a start in life? I too, would like to be the old-shoe guy who so fearlessly risked panicking five million people by setting off the midnight air-raid sirens because the White Sox had finally won a pennant.

I too wish to defend my city from people who keep saying it is crooked. In what other city can you be so sure a judge will keep his word for five hundred dollars? What's so crooked about that? I'm tired of hearing detractors of my city say it is br*oo*-tul. For in what other city, head held high, sweating, laughing, all of that, can you get homicide reduced to manslaughter and manslaughter to a felony and felony to a misdemeanor? What's so br*oo*-tul about *that?* What do you want, for God's sake? Your gun back?

"We have to keep Chicago strong and America mighty!" I heard His Honor proclaim before sentencing the girl with a record for addiction, "A year and a day! Take her away!"

Blinking out of the window of an Ogden Avenue trolley at the sunlight she hadn't seen for almost a year, "I guess it was lucky I done that time," the girl philosophized, "Chicago still looks pretty strong and America looks mighty mighty."

Still nobody seems to be laughing.

Since this essay first indicated that we are engaged in horrors as well as marvels here, horrors have multiplied with marvels. Now we have among us the affluent bubble-gum snapper, the man so disconnected from reality that he pays fifty dollars for a key with a bunny engraved on it in order to obtain recognition of his personality as being, officially, that of a Playboy.

And what if, having paid his fifty and dressing for the occasion, he should gain an entrée that will endow him with the assurance that he is different from the rest—only to find the room empty. Nobody in it at all? Did somebody snicker out there?

Perhaps the reason our thinking has shifted from the informal attitude of a society that makes allowances, to the more rigid, legalistic "he brought it all on himself" attitude, derives from the isolation of so many Americans, bubble-gum snappers and key-club cats alike. For the isolated man is a loveless man. Although his children may call him Papa and go through the gestures of love, they yet can't reach him. This isolation is common enough to justify calling it The American Disease and is directly related to the lack of creativity in this city; that was once America's creative center.

For the fraudulence essential to successful merchandising becomes pervasive, so that the class which is economically empowered becomes emotionally hollowed.

This would account for the fact that every enduring portrait in American fiction is that of a man or woman outside the upper middle-class. From Ahab to Ethan Frome and Willie Loman, Hawthorne's branded woman to Blanche du Bois, all are people who, living without alternatives, are thus forced to feel life all the way. While the attempts at middle-class portraiture, such as Marjorie Morningstar, fade as fast as last year's bestseller.

Well, no use to call out the hook-and-ladders. So long as Jerry Lewis Jr. is doing such a good job of handling children's diseases for us and Sammy Davis Jr. has integration in hand, I see no reason why our city should not be proud in giving America Hugh Hefner to handle sex.

As I once heard a thoughtful young woman put it during a matinee at Chicago Theater where Sinatra was appearing in person—

"Spit on me, Frankie! I'm in the very front row!"

As the girl was in the second balcony, I thought the idea a little unusual.

In the decade since *Chicago: City on the Make* appeared, it has gained pertinence. At that time it was a prose-poem about my home-town; nothing more.

It was received unfavorably, locally, and I was disappointed when the editor who had solicited it took fright. I had assumed he was more than one more New York hustler looking for something for nothing; but he was not. The book went under the counters; not the first book to be lost by an editor too timid to stand by his own thinking.

Under the counters, yet not lost. A translation by Jean-Paul Sartre gained the essay readers abroad, and the present re-publication is largely indebted to overseas interest.

For the essay made the assumption that, in times when the levers of power are held by those who have lost the will to act honestly, it is those who have been excluded from the privileges of our society, and left only its horrors, who forge new levers by which to return honesty to us. The present resolution of a new generation of Negro men and women, now forcing the return of the American promise of dignity for all, sustains the assumption.

And as the time grows short for us to recognize that

such dignity is not the prerogative of the economically empowered, the time for recognition that the claim of the peoples of Cuba and South America is equally just, is yet shorter.

This essay carried the implication that the castaways of western civilization were not restless through instruction from devils in The Kremlin; but from the instruction of the hearts of men everywhere where men wish to own their own lives. Present events justify the implication.

And if the essay can to any degree belie those dangerous fantasies, now rising like a threatening pall between Belmont, Massachusetts, and Glenview, Illinois, it shall have served our curious times more purposefully than by its original conception.

Chicago, May, 1961
Nelson Algren

Notes

Page x
With heart at rest. . . . I love thee, infamous city! Excerpt from Charles
Baudelaire's poem "Draft Epilogue" for the 1861 edition of *Flowers of
Evil.*

Page 9
The Hustlers People working a con game or other illegitimate enter-
prise.

Page 10
secondhand Used goods.
marked-down For sale at a lower price.
portage A trail between waterways where Native Americans and fur
traders would carry their goods and canoes from one waterway to another. Chicago exists due to its portage between the Great Lakes/North
Atlantic and the Mississippi River trading systems.
Pottawattomies Variant spelling of Potawatomi, Native American tribe
which inhabited the Chicago area; removed by the 1833 Treaty of
Chicago.

Page 11

vermilion   Red dye; a common early trade item.

roll boulevards   In the nineteenth century, Chicago solved some of the problems inherent in building a city on a swamp by raising the grade of the streets. Later, the Burnham Plan of 1909 included a system of boulevards to connect the city's parks and the lakefront.

roll its dark river uphill   Reversal of the Chicago River in 1900. Due to its role as the city's sewer, the River polluted Lake Michigan, the source of the city's drinking water, causing frequent epidemics of cholera and other waterborne diseases. The Chicago Sanitary and Ship Canal was dug, causing the River to quite literally flow uphill.

yankee   New Englander.

voyageur   French fur trader.

Irish   Chicago's first large immigrant group, brought to the city to dig canals and later build railroads.

Dutch   Germans; Chicago's largest group of immigrants.

Indian agents   Government agents responsible for dealing with Native American tribes.

halfbreed and quarterbreed. . . .   Algren appropriated imagery and language in this passage from a description of Chicago by English traveler Charles LaTrobe, who witnessed the signing of the 1833 Treaty of Chicago which called for the removal of the Potawatomi.

Sauganash   The city's first hotel/tavern, owned by legendary early settler Mark Beaubien and named in honor of Billy Caldwell, an Indian agent of half-Mohawk, half-British descent. "Sauganash" was the Potawatomi term for English-speaking Canadians, and Caldwell's nickname. The hotel was not a barracks, but LaTrobe described it thus.

Page 12

peltries   Uncured animal skins.

grog   Hot whiskey drink.

derringer   A small one- or two-shot handgun.

Paid the Pottawattomies off in cash. . . .   Reference to the 1833 Treaty of Chicago, which called for the removal of all native tribes from Illinois, and the financial skullduggery which ensued. The deal which made Chicago possible was its first hustle.

Balaban and Katz   Operators of a large movie theater chain.

Generous Sport   In Chicago's first directory, in 1839, one William Rogers listed his profession as "the generous sport," i.e., a gambler.

blackleg   Swindler.

coonskin roisterer   Frontiersman, so called for their caps made of raccoon skin.

Long Knives   Indian term for white men, especially U.S. Army officers.

bondsmen   Indentured servants or slaves.

bounty jumpers   Men who had taken a cash bounty for joining various units of the Union Army during the Civil War, and then deserted with the money; some men repeated this process many times.

Page 13

jump bond   Flee the law.

the city's very first jailbird. . . .   In the first city directory, one Richard Harper is described as "'Old Harper', vag[rant]"; George White is listed as "City crier." This incident suggests the racism and disregard for the law present in Chicago from its very inception.

two bits   Twenty-five cents.

Do-Gooders   Reform-minded people.

village squares   Immigrants to Chicago from small midwestern towns; the opposite of hustlers.

pokey   Jail.

Page 14

Jane Addams   Nobel Peace Prize Laureate, social reformer, founder of Hull-House, and crusader for the rights of workers, women, African Americans, and immigrants; a secular saint in American history. For Algren, Addams represented individuals who stand up for their political beliefs regardless of the personal consequences—her unrelenting pacifism, which continued throughout the patriotic war fervor of World War I, cost Addams dearly in terms of her national standing, but she did not abandon her principles.

two outs . . . four   Each side should, according to the rules of baseball, get three outs per inning.

Big Bill Thompson   Republican Mayor from 1915 to 1923 and from 1927 to 1931. A municipal booster and builder of public works, Thompson won by bringing African-American voters into a coalition with white ethnics against conservative nativist politicians and civic leaders. Thompson's *laissez-faire* attitude towards Prohibition laws reflected the pro-repeal opinions of his political base, and enabled his conservative foes to label him, perhaps inaccurately, as a lackey of organized crime.

Al Capone   The quintessential mobster, Boss of the Chicago Outfit at the height of Prohibition-era gangland violence. His actual reign was relatively short, but like many Chicago characters, he was a publicity hound, and so has been mythologized in countless books, films, and television series. Until the coming of Michael Jordan, Capone symbolized Chicago worldwide.

reform mayor   William Dever, Democratic mayor from 1923 to 1927. His election and crackdown on organized crime forced Capone to move his headquarters to the West Side suburb of Cicero, but actually increased urban disorder and violence, as attempts to enforce Prohibition laws were met with resistance.

Prohibition   The period from 1919 to 1933 when the sale of liquor was prohibited in the United States.

Law-and-Order League   The earlier of two conservative organizations which protested against public immorality, especially in the Levee district but in relation to saloon culture in general. Joseph Medill, publisher of the *Chicago Tribune,* was elected mayor with its support and served one contentious and unpopular term from 1871 to 1873.

Page 15

shut Sunday beer halls . . . Beer-on-Sunday Party   One of the more dramatic instances of conflict between Chicago's conservative Protestant New Englanders and mostly Catholic European immigrants. Medill enforced Chicago's laws requiring saloons and beer halls to close on Sundays, which, before the advent of the forty-hour workweek, were a worker's only day off.

ruins of the great fire   The Great Chicago Fire of 8–10 October 1871. Most of the city, including sidewalks and some roads, was built of wood, dry after a long drought. Discredited legend holds that Mrs. O'Leary's cow kicked over a lantern in a barn on West DeKoven Street; strong winds spread the flames north. Three and a half square miles of the city were burnt, over 300 people killed, and two hundred million dollars in property lost. This pivotal moment in Chicago's history not only attracted thousands of immigrant workers to rebuild, it wiped the urban slate clean, enabling the city to move to the forefront of modern industry, urban planning, and architecture.

eight-hour day   Crucial issue in the conflict between capital and labor.

Gipsy Smith   Evangelist who led protests against patrons and owners in the Levee vice district.

old Levee   Chicago's notorious First Ward vice district, presided over by corrupt politicians and police from the mid-nineteenth century until

1914. The Levee existed because many people believed that "victimless" crimes like drinking, drugs, gambling, and prostitution, based on "weaknesses of the flesh," were an inevitable part of human nature and could never be wholly eradicated. Given this attitude, it was thought better to keep such vice in a particular area, away from middle class districts, where it could be controlled and regulated to some degree.

Page 16

W.C.T.U. The Women's Christian Temperance Union.

Old Cap Streeter George Wellington "Cap" Streeter ran his steamboat aground off the shore of Lake Michigan north of the River in 1886; dumping between his ship and the shore gradually created a landfill. He declared the area independent of Illinois, Cook County, and Chicago, named it the District of Michigan, and sold plots of land in what soon became a vice district. In 1918, after numerous battles with the law—in court with lawyers and out of court with guns—he was finally evicted from what is now known as Streeterville.

Legion of Decency Roman Catholic organization which rated films by moral standards.

Lieutenant Fulmer, Preston Bradley Crusaders against vice.

Epworth League Methodist reform group.

Emile Coué French pharmacist who invented a quack form of psychotherapy, Couéism, based on repeating the phrase "Every day, and in every way, I am becoming better and better."

Dwight L. Moody Evangelist, founder of the church which still bears his name on the Near North Side, crusader against alcohol, dancing, the theatre, Sunday business openings and the Sunday papers.

million-candled Candle-power, a measure of brightness.

Old Fitzgerald . . . Four Roses Liquor brand names.

arc-lamps Street lights.

Are You a Christian?

Pages 18–19

John the Baptist . . . Black Jack Yattaw . . . Duffy the Goat . . . Reed Waddell Algren singles out these criminals—notorious pimps, thieves, pushers, killers and confidence men—due to their colorful characters and the brazenness of their transgressions. Yattaw, for instance, ran a bumboat, a floating bar/brothel/gambling den, which he docked on the river, filled with customers, and then sailed out into the lake where the city's laws could not be enforced. Duffy the Goat was so named for his habit, in brawls, of headbutting his opponents in the midriff. The victims of the con artists, or bunko men like Waddell, often included prominent and unsuspecting visitors to the city, such as American diplomat Charles Francis Adams and Anglo-Irish writer Oscar Wilde, both swindled in 1882.

gold-brick fraud   A confidence game where the con man convinces his mark that a brick is solid gold when in fact it is mostly brass, with only a plug of gold for testing.

Page 20

Mickey Finn   Infamous Levee saloon-keeper. In his Lone Star Saloon, he created a knockout drink in order to rob patrons. His name has entered the American language as a term for such a drink.

Hinky Dink Kenna   Michael Kenna, nicknamed for his short stature; famously corrupt Alderman of the First Ward and boss, along with Bathhouse John Coughlin, of the Levee District.

apache   Native American tribe; slang for criminal.

brigand   Bold criminal.

Gold Coast   Affluent neighborhood, home to many upper-class reformers.

free lunches   The practice, begun in Chicago, of saloons providing free food for customers who bought a drink. Anti-liquor activists considered the free lunch an immoral enticement; even the politically progressive Upton Sinclair depicted the free lunch as such in his 1906 novel of the stockyards, *The Jungle*. But for many workers and the poor, the free lunch might be their only available meal.

Workingman's Exchange   Kenna's saloon at Clark and Van Buren, so called because like many saloons, it acted as a union organizing hall as well as a place to drink.

missions   Missionary societies which feed the poor, but require them to listen to proselytizing preachers before being fed and housed.

Page 21

cribs   Brothels.

Lucy Page Gaston   Chicago anti-tobacco reformer and founder of the 20th-century version of the Law and Order League. She dubbed the cigarette a "coffin nail," and was famous for her publicity stunts, such as invading brothels in the Levee to accuse the madams of sending their girls to hell—for smoking, not prostitution.

Bathhouse John   John Coughlin, partner of Hinky Dink Kenna. One of Chicago's most colorfully overdressed and corrupt politicians, he was so nicknamed because he had worked in a bathhouse, a common occupation in the days when most tenement homes lacked indoor plumbing.

Page 22

rogues' circus   The Chicago City Council, a legislative body renowned for its long history of rhetorical grandstanding, financial skullduggery, blatant boodling, and unparalleled political corruption.

hopheads   Drunks or drug addicts.

coneroos   Confidence men.

fancy-men   Men, especially pimps, who live off the earnings of women.

dips   Pickpockets.

hipsters   Someone hip, in the know.

First Ward Ball   Annual political fundraiser for Kenna and Coughlin, attended primarily by the Levee's criminal element and thrill-seekers, and hence an affront to Chicago's respectable citizens.

private zoo   One of Coughlin's extravagances, paid for with boodle and built on his ranch in Colorado Springs, Colorado.

tweeds   The classier dress style of the generation of hustlers which followed Coughlin.

"The cult of money . . ."   Many visitors to Chicago commented on the city's rampant greed; we have not been able to identify the exact source of this passage, and Algren may have coined it himself by conflating several such comments.

Page 23

Tuesday Night Lineup   The Chicago Police Department practice of rounding up the usual suspects to be identified by victims of and witnesses to crimes.

Bronzeville   Chicago's African-American district, created by real estate covenants which limited blacks to this one overcrowded and slowly expanding area. Here Chicagoans built their Black Metropolis, second only to New York's Harlem as a center for African-American culture and business.

Billy Sunday   Evangelist and former major-league baseball player. He found that Chicago was one town he could not shut down.

Page 24

White Sox   Chicago's American League professional baseball team, generally supported by Southsiders. Algren was a lifelong fan of the Sox.

Cubs   Chicago's National League professional baseball team, generally supported by Northsiders. Perennial and proverbial losers.

King Oliver . . . Dave Tough   Cornetist King Oliver's Creole Jazz Band brought radical innovators in American music like trumpeter Louis Armstrong and drummers Dodds and Tough to Chicago venues like the Lincoln Gardens Bandstand.

old soaks' goat's nests   Slum dwellings of drunks.

Page 25

Jackson Park Express   Elevated ("El") train which would skip certain stations.

patronage . . . like a flower   The practice of giving municipal jobs to political operatives in return for votes and partisan work throughout the year, especially on election day. This quasi-feudal and corruptible practice, where individuals owed loyalty to whomever was above them in the hierarchy, was the foundation of Chicago's Democratic machine.

monstrous forges of Gary and East Chicago   Centers of steel production.

Page 26

The Loop   Chicago's central business and government district, now defined by the Elevated tracks; originally called the Loop due to the streetcar lines which circled it before the construction of the El.

welter of industrial towns   Neighborhoods built up around factories.

No railroad passes through. . . .   A source of considerable profit for baggage handlers, taxis, hotels and others, as no passenger or freight train could bypass the city. In a sense, Chicago is still a portage.

the Constellations   Passenger planes.

Rogers Park   Chicago's northeasternmost neighborhood; hence, metaphorically at least, far removed from Bronzeville.

Lincoln Park   The city's first graveyard, transformed into one of the country's great urban parks in the 1860s; also the neighborhood west of the park.

Outer Drive   Lake Shore Drive.

those suburbs   Affluent suburbs, on the North Shore.

Town and Country   Magazine chronicling the fashions, homes, and lifestyles of socialites and the well-to-do.

kapok   Horsehair, used as carpet padding and furniture stuffing.

Page 27
Reader's Digest   Conservative middlebrow magazine.

The Silver-Colored Yesterday
Page 30
Cottage Grove . . . Seventy-first   Far South Side streets of Algren's boyhood neighborhood.
Shoeless Joe Jackson   White Sox leftfielder and owner of the third highest career batting average in baseball history. Jackson is considered by many to be a tragic figure in the Black Sox scandal, when seven players on the 1919 White Sox conspired with gamblers to throw the World Series to the vastly inferior Cincinnati Reds. For $10,000 per man, shortstop Swede Risberg and first baseman Chick Gandil ensured gamblers that with the help of pitcher Eddie Cicotte they could lose the Series. Shoeless Joe Jackson, utility infielder Ed McMullin, centerfielder Hap Felsch and pitcher Lefty Williams agreed to go along with the fix; third baseman Buck Weaver knew of the deal but refused to cooperate. The men were found innocent of conspiracy charges in a Cook County trial in which signed confessions somehow disappeared from a judge's chambers. But all eight were banned from professional baseball for life in 1920 by newly named Baseball Commissioner Kenesaw Mountain Landis. For Algren, this event has dual significance. It is yet another example of potential greatness squandered due to greed, as players tossed their honor away for money. But, more importantly perhaps, it shows the great American double standard between capital and labor, as the owners and front-office men of the White Sox—who knew of the fix and did nothing—were not punished, while the players lost their livelihoods.
Ty Cobb   Perhaps the greatest hitter in baseball history, Cobb played from 1905 to 1928.
Carl Wanderer   World War I veteran, hanged in 1921. Wanderer hired a skid row derelict to stage a robbery, where his wife would be killed; Wanderer double-crossed his accomplice (whose identity has never been discovered) and murdered him as well.
John Dillinger   Bank robber, killer and the first Public Enemy Number One; shot to death in Chicago outside the Biograph Theatre on Lincoln Avenue by the FBI in 1934.
Terrible Tommy O'Connor   Minor Chicago hoodlum, major mythic figure. He gained fame when, sentenced to death for killing Chicago detective

Patrick O'Neil, he escaped from the Old County Jail on Dearborn Street in 1921. Despite a manhunt, he was never recaptured.
Saturday Evening Blade   Local weekly sensationalistic tabloid.

Page 31
white hope   A white contender for a boxing title; coined after the dominance of black fighters in the heavyweight division.
puss   Face.

Page 32
barflies   Drunks, especially those who hang out in bars to cadge drinks.
banneger   A strong punch.
White City   Amusement park on the South Side, which often staged prize fights.

Page 33
St. Columbanus   Roman Catholic church near Algren's boyhood home.
beer-cork hunting   Corks used to seal beer bottles, which often had brand logos burnt into them.
"Be my little . . . ."   Title lyrics of 1912 song by Stanley Murphy and Henry I. Marshall.
Louisville slugger bat   Bat used by most major-league players.
Comiskey Park program   A publication sold on game days listing the players in a ballgame, allowing for fans to make notations tracking the plays. Comiskey Park was the home field of the White Sox, and the program acts as physical and textual proof of his claim to have attended a game in person.
bleachers   Cheap seats, usually beyond the outfield walls.

Page 34
shutting out   Not allowing your opponent to score.
Wrigley Field   Home of the Cubs.
fayvrut   Favorite.
sprouts   Children.
Edison victrola   Early record player.
local loyalty board   Algren depicts the Black Sox scandal as a metaphor for McCarthyism and the House Un-American Activities Committee Hearings. For Algren, the players who were—perhaps unjustly—run out of the game parallel the writers, artists, filmmakers,

actors, and academics whose careers—and sometimes lives—were destroyed by blacklisting and anti-communist witch hunts.

prospect Ballplayer with great potential.

chairman Joseph McCarthy, Republican senator from Wisconsin who made his career by instigating an anti-communist witch hunt.

Charley Hollocher Cubs shortstop.

t'row righty Throw right-handed.

Grover Cleveland Alexander Hall-of-Fame Cubs pitcher. With 373 career wins, he is acknowledged as one of baseball's all-time greatest pitchers.

Bill Killefer Cubs catcher.

Page 35

called third strike A strikeout where the player does not swing, but the umpire judges the ball a strike; an ignominious out.

umpire Baseball's on-field adjudicators.

The Committee Another reference to the McCarthy hearings.

Page 36

coal shed roof The game would have been taking place in an alley, where buildings like coal sheds and other obstacles would have been part of the "field."

bloopers Weakly hit balls.

line drive A strongly hit ball.

Reds . . . October Here Algren juxtaposes the Black Sox Scandal, the Russian Revolution, the Red Scare of 1919, and the Cold War anti-communist witch hunts.

guilt of association . . . charge was conspiracy During the HUAC hearings, merely associating with anyone accused of un-American activities— i.e., anyone with leftist political beliefs, at the time or in the past—produced the presumption of guilt and conspiracy.

Hoodhood Gangsters.

Comiskey Many mythologizers of the Black Sox scandal, including Algren, blame team owner Comiskey's tightfistedness for driving the players into the arms of the gamblers.

Page 37

at bat Turn at the plate to hit.

caught sleeping Picked off when not paying attention on base; an ignominious out.

wild peg Inaccurate throw.

thrun Threw.

played bum Sold out to gamblers.

Tobey of that committee Conservative Republican Charles Tobey, senator from New Hampshire from 1939 to 1953.

What kind of American are you anyhow? Perhaps the key question in the book, as McCarthyism postulated that certain political ideas or personal loyalties were essentially un-American.

Page 38

perfec' perfect

wit' With.

Page 39

Rothstein Arnold Rothstein, New York gangster and gambler reputed to have fixed the 1919 World Series from safely behind the scenes; basis for the character of Meyer Wolfsheim in F. Scott Fitzgerald's *The Great Gatsby* (1925).

"Svenska" Swedish for "Swedish."

shiner Black eye.

pitch in . . . victory Bribe the other team to lose.

sandlot Informal baseball diamond.

Love is for Barflies
Page 42

rap Dismiss or disrespect.

joint Place.

crosstown . . . Armitage Avenue barns Ticket allowing one to transfer between streetcar lines; a large transfer point was at the intersection of Armitage and Milwaukee Avenues.

Page 43

fix Local political powerbroker.

the Hoosier fireman Eugene Victor Debs, locomotive fireman (the man who stoked the steam engine's boiler with coal), renowned orator, and labor leader who went from being City Clerk of Terre Haute to five-time Socialist candidate for United States President. Debs began his political career committed to peaceful employer/employee cooperation, but was eventually radicalized by capitalist indifference to workers' needs and by the violence often used to break strikes.

Page 44
"I despise your . . . ." Statement made to the court by Louis Lingg, one of the Haymarket Martyrs. Lingg killed himself in prison.
Why Not? Name of the brothel.
wardheeler Corrupt local politician.
Milwaukee Avenue Main Street of Chicago's Polish community.
straphangers Commuters.
ginmills Low-class bars.

Page 45
protean Changeable.
peg the rents Set the price of housing. The high demand for apartments in Bronzeville, caused by overcrowding, enabled real estate agents to raise rents.

Page 46
"If you're white. . . ." Lyrics from "Black, Brown and White" by Chicago bluesman Big Bill Broonzy.
greyboy Slang for an African American.
Senator Douglas Democratic U.S. senator from Illinois, Paul Douglas was personally liberal, and fought for Civil Rights in Washington—but that was far away from the realities of the South Side.
King Levinsky Boxer.

Page 47
Sunset Boulevard Street in Los Angeles.
pansies Gay men.
pekes Pekinese breed lapdogs.
Truman Capote Fashionable writer and fashion plate.
Flair Fashion magazine.

Page 48
State . . . Clark . . . Madison Streets notorious as either redlight districts, skid rows, or both.
parlor-cars Expensive train accommodations.
all-night beacon . . . stratoliners Lights on tall buildings meant to guide airplanes.
heavy shouldered laugher Reference to Sandburg's poem "Chicago."

Page 49
cocksure Overconfident.

Bright Faces of Tomorrow
Page 52
Vachel Lindsay Springfield, Illinois-born poet known for "Congo," "General William Booth Enters Into Heaven," "Abraham Lincoln Walks at Midnight" and his tribute to Altgeld, entitled "The Eagle That Is Forgotten." Along with other writers, architects, and artists, he was a key player in the Chicago Renaissance.
Masters Edgar Lee Masters, lawyer, historian, Chicago Renaissance novelist and poet best known for *The Spoon River Anthology*.
Edna Millay Edna St. Vincent Millay, Modernist poet.

Page 53
Rush Street Poet and literary critic Lawrence Lipton, a close friend of Algren, lived in an apartment on Rush Street, where leftist writers gathered in the 1930s and '40s.
Wright Richard Wright, friend of Algren and author best known for his novel *Native Son* (1940). Algren fell out with Wright over his decision to move to France to escape American racism.
Café Flore Paris cafe and writers' hangout, known to Algren through his affair with Simone de Beauvoir.
Herb Graffis *Chicago Sun Times* golf writer.

Page 54
Mencken In 1920—not 1930—H. L. Mencken declared in "The Literary Capital of the United States," that there was "not a single novelist [. . .] deserving of a civilized reader's notice—who has not sprung from the Middle Empire that has Chicago for its capital."
Bix Beiderbecke Jazz cornetist from Iowa, mentored by Louis Armstrong. Beiderbecke brought jazz to many white audiences, but died young.
Mary Garden Opera singer whose performance of *Salome* scandalized Chicago's moralists.
Billy Petrolle Boxer.
Gene Field Journalist and poet, best known for children's verse.
Dreiser Novelist Theodore Dreiser, renowned for *Sister Carrie* (1900) and *An American Tragedy* (1925). His naturalist style, depiction of Chicago,

social conscience, and commitment to telling the truth regardless of the consequences, influenced Algren profoundly.

Anderson   Chicago Renaissance novelist and short-story writer Sherwood Anderson, best known for *Winesburg, Ohio* (1919).

Battling Nelson . . . Davey Day   Boxers.

No-Hit Charley Robertson   White Sox hurler; pitched a perfect game—a contest in which no batter reaches base, one of the rarest feats in baseball—on 30 April 1922.

Page 55

Bismarck Gardens   Beer garden of the pre-Prohibition era.

Marigold   Jazz club located at the intersection of Broadway, Grace, and Halsted streets.

Sam T. Jack's Burlesque   Probably a reference to a Sam T. Jack's Creole Show, the first African-American artistic group to produce musicals which broke with the minstrel tradition.

Globe on Desplaines   Probably a jazz club or theatre.

Chicora   Freighter which made a late-season run from South Haven, Michigan to Milwaukee in January 1895; overtaken by a severe storm, it sank with all hands. Algren family legend held that his uncle, a lakeship boathand, had been kicked off the crew of the ship for fighting prior to its last voyage. While this reference relates to Algren's family, it also connects to his constant concern for workers: the owners and captain of the ship knew that a January crossing was perilous, but took the chance in hopes of profit.

open-front hacks   Taxis where the driver was not enclosed.

jack handle   Metal bar for jacking up a vehicle.

Sam Insull   Utilities magnate. Insull is another example, for Algren, of how the rich and powerful can get away with crimes while the poor cannot: Insull was tried three times—for fraud, violation of bankruptcy laws, and embezzlement—and was acquitted each time.

Great Man Shires   Art Shires, part-time White Sox first baseman from 1928 to 1930. Nicknamed "Art the Great," Shires had, at best, a marginal major-league career.

overbraided brass   Military high command.

Page 57

Tribune   Chicago newspaper, long a voice of reactionary conservatism.

Frank Harris   Popular progressive British novelist, better known for his scandalous behavior rather than his novel criticizing America for the miscarriage of justice at Haymarket, *The Bomb* (1920).

gangway   Walkway between two buildings, leading from the sidewalk to a back yard or alley; where lower-class prostitutes would conduct business.

Robert Hutchins   So-called Boy President of the University of Chicago, who eliminated the school's football team and created their "great books" educational system.

Robert Morss Lovett   Professor and political activist who opposed racism and imperialism.

Hearst   William Randolph Hearst, arch-conservative newspaper publisher and inventor of yellow journalism.

McCormick   Either Cyrus McCormick, inventor of the mechanical reaper and industrialist famous for the strike against his plant in 1886, which led to Haymarket; or Robert McCormick, conservative ideologue and publisher of the *Chicago Tribune*.

Page 58

Big Bluff   Confidence game.

Congressman Lincoln . . . Polk   Abraham Lincoln, U.S. Representative from Illinois from 1847 to 1849. Polk was President during the Mexican War, which many Americans saw as blatant imperialism.

Springfield   Capital of Illinois.

Page 59

"gooks"   Disparaging term for people of Asian descent.

1917   Algren here sets up a parallel between the beginning of the Korean War and the veterans of the First World War.

geeks   Carnival performers whose acts consist of biting the head off a live chicken or snake.

winoes . . . ginsoaks   Drunks.

dingbats   Half-wits.

D Plus One, D Plus Two   One or two days after D-day, the invasion of Normandy by the Allies on 6 June 1944.

G.I. issue   Government Issue.

Page 60

mulligan   Stew made by hobos with whatever ingredients are handy.

derail   Adulterated alcohol.

goon squads   Enforcers employed by industrialists to break strikes.

turn on the night   Although this might appear to be an error for "turn on the light," it appears thus in both the first edition and the *Holiday* version; a suggestion of Algren's attitudes towards many issues.

No More Giants
Page 62
torpedoes . . . coneroos   Small-time crooks and conmen.
.38   A handgun.
six-ouncers   Boxing gloves.
"City of the big shoulders"   Line 5 of Sandburg's "Chicago."
four standing . . . eight hour day . . . when bomb was thrown and the deed was done   The Haymarket Martyrs. On 2 May 1886, two workers striking for the eight-hour day were killed by police at the McCormick Reaper Works. A protest rally was held two days later at Chicago's Haymarket, at the intersection of Desplaines and Randolph. After what even Mayor Carter Harrison described as a peaceful demonstration, Chicago police charged into the crowd, and someone threw a bomb, killing police officer Matthias Degan. In the ensuing battle, seven police officers were killed, along with an unknown number of protesters. Chicago police rounded up hundreds of people purely on the grounds of their ethnicity, politics, or labor activism, and eventually eight men were convicted of conspiracy, despite the fact that even the prosecution conceded that they did not actually throw the bomb or directly encourage anyone to do so. For conservatives, the bomb thrown at Haymarket represented foreign-bred anarchy and lawlessness, and the trial restored order. For Algren and others, the fact that eight men were convicted and four hanged for their political beliefs unmasks the hypocrisy and violence at the heart of the American system.

Page 63
Grover Cleveland . . . Altgeld . . . McCormick the Reaper   Law partner of Clarence Darrow, John Peter Altgeld was the reform-minded Democratic governor of Illinois from 1893 to 1897. He sacrificed his political career by pardoning the Haymarket conspirators sentenced to life in prison. Altgeld also reformed the prison system, improved public schools, and stood up for labor rights in his opposition to U.S. President Cleveland's decision to send federal troops into the Pullman and McCormick Reaper strikes.
houseman   Dealer or croupier in an illegal card or dice game.

Page 64

sheet a foot long   "Rap sheet"; list of crimes one has committed or been accused of.

C-note; C   One hundred dollars.

Big Bill Haywood   Miner and leading labor activist, affiliated with the International Workers of the World, Haywood was jailed for calling a strike during World War I; while out on bail, he jumped bond and fled to Moscow, where he died in 1928. Half of his ashes are buried there, the other half near the monument to the Haymarket Martyrs.

First of May   May Day, the International Labor Holiday, inspired by Haymarket and other events in Chicago.

cornice-makers, tin-roofers and lumber-shovers   Groups active in the early Chicago labor movement and at Haymarket; oddly, all defunct trades by Algren's day.

race riots   In July 1919, Eugene Williams, an African American, drowned off of the 29th Street Beach. He could not come to shore due to a stone-throwing fight between black and white youths, and rumors that he had been stoned to death sparked five days of widespread violence. Twenty-three blacks and fifteen whites were killed; hundreds were injured.

professional anti-Semites   Many North Shore suburbs excluded Jews.

Page 65

33, 45, 78 rpm   Speeds at which different sorts of phonograph records rotated.

Barnum-and-Bailey   Consummate American showmen, and conmen, they ran America's largest and most successful circus.

Yellow Kid Weil   Famed conman, known for his sophisticated dress, high living, and reputation for cheating only the rich.

Gorgeous George   Flamboyant professional wrestler.

Sewell Avery   Chairman of Chicago retail giant Montgomery Ward, and a vociferous opponent of labor rights.

Elizabeth Dilling   Anti-communist, anti-Semitic pamphleteer.

Joe Beauharnais   White supremacist who distributed pamphlets calling for an armed uprising against African Americans. He was arrested under an Illinois law forbidding the defamation of groups, and his case went to the U.S. Supreme Court, which held that the law did not violate the First Amendment.

Botsy Connors   Probably William "Botchy" Connors, local political boss.

Shipwreck Kelly   Flagpole sitter.

The Great I Am   Christian sect which operates a chain of reading rooms promoting its claims.

Oliver J. Dragon   The dragon puppet on the *Kukla, Fran and Ollie* children's television show.

Only-One-on-Earth Colonel McGooseneck   Colonel Robert McCormick, arch-conservative publisher of the *Tribune*.

boners   Errors.

10–8   In the fourth game of the 1929 World Series, Cub centerfielder Hack Wilson lost a fly ball in the sun, and the Philadelphia Athletics scored 10 runs after 2 outs in the seventh inning to win the game 10–8.

Where somebody . . . second   Here Algren allows his dislike of the Cubs to rewrite history. The direct reference is to Merkle's Boner, one of the more famous events in baseball history. In the Polo Grounds during the 1908 season, Fred Merkle of the New York Giants failed to touch second base at the end of a game, allowing the Cubs to claim victory by forfeit because a mob of New York fans stormed the field. The Cubs eventually won the replay and the pennant over the Giants by that one game—but the incident did not take place in Chicago, and the Cubs (for once) were on the winning side.

Page 66

Mayor Kelly   Edward Kelly, Democratic mayor of Chicago from 1933 to 1947.

rights of Owners and rights of Man   Reference to the American obsession with property rights, in opposition to the Enlightenment concept of the Natural Rights of Man. In *The Man With the Golden Arm*, Algren describes America as "the one land where ownership and virtue are one."

Philadelphia first baseman   Ed Waitkus, shot by Ruth Steinhagen in the Edgewater Beach hotel in 1949. Bernard Malamud adapted this incident in his novel *The Natural* (1952).

newsies   Boys or men who sold newspapers on the street.

pinboys   Boys employed setting pins in bowling alleys.

Montgomery-Ward sleepwalkers   Shoppers at a department store.

Garfield Park Local   El train which would make all stops.

university's faculty protest   Reference to the liberal politics of many University of Chicago faculty, and their ignorance of the University administration's complicity in the racial segregation around Hyde Park.

Page 67

real estate . . . covenants   Chicago housing segregation was not law; an agreement among real estate operators perpetuated racial division.

carillons   Church bells.

"The slums take their revenge"   Assessment of the 1919 Chicago Race Riots made by the white-haired poet Carl Sandburg.

Page 69

Lorado Taft   Sculptor, best known for *Fountain of Time,* a grim sculpture at the west end of the Midway Plaisance on the University of Chicago campus.

Harvester, the sleeping car, the Bessemer Process   Three of Chicago's key industries. Here Algren associates steelmaking, the Pullman Company, and Cyrus McCormick's mechanical harvester as emblematic of industry: all were sites of major battles between labor and capital.

Nobody Knows where O'Connor Went
Page 72

extry-hawking newsie   Newspaper vendor selling ("hawking") special extra editions of the papers.

carbarn   Streetcar garage.

Englewood Local   Train making all stops.

Page 73

press box   Seats for newspaper reporters at a ballgame.

Thirty-fifth   Street on which Comiskey Park is located.

Page 74

straw kelly   Summer hat.

Happy-Days-Are-Here-Again   Song by Jack Yellen and Milton Ager; feel-good theme song of FDR's first presidential campaign.

It's only a paper moon   Song by lyricist E. Y. Harburg and composer Harold Arlen.

Joe Felso   Generic term for anyone; the average Chicagoan.

"Laughing . . . battle"   Line 20 of Sandburg's "Chicago."

Page 75

Ford in his future   Ford advertising slogan.

The jail . . . gone   Parsons and the other Haymarket Martyrs were hanged at the old Cook County Jail, on Illinois Street between Clark and Dear-

born, demolished after the new County Jail opened in 1929.
lonely shaft Statue commemorating Haymarket.

Page 76

Eastland One of Chicago's most famous disasters. On 24 July 1915, the steamer *Eastland*, moored in the Chicago River for a summer excursion with 2,572 employees of the Western Electric Company, capsized due to overloading, killing 844 people.

"My God, How the Money Rolls In" Satirical song, praising the profitability of various illegal occupations, from prostitute to bootlegger.

"Brother, Can You Spare a Dime?" Song by lyricist E. Y. Harburg and composer George Gershwin. Harburg was a target of the HUAC investigations.

Southside jukes Bar with a jukebox for entertainment.

hockshop Pawn shop.

penny arcade Gameroom with pinball machines and other amusements.

shooting gallery Location where intravenous drug abusers shoot up.

Afterword In this essay, originally published as a preface to the second edition of *City on the Make* in 1961, Algren does two things. First, he responds to the civic critics of the first edition who attacked the book as unbalanced and misguided, a slanted portrait of Chicago. Perhaps more importantly, he also asserts his definition of literature as being made on "any occasion that a challenge is put to the legal apparatus by conscience in touch with humanity." Through a series of legal metaphors, Algren argues that identification with the outsider and the criminal is essential if we are to maintain our own humanity. He rejects the growing academic conservative consensus that literature should primarily attend to aesthetic or formal concerns; instead he argues that literature must be considered a politically and socially engaged practice.

Page 83

retarded Kilgallens Dorothy Kilgallen, TV celebrity and columnist, syndicated by the Hearst papers.

Page 85

Chicagoese Da way we tawk in Chicawgo.

Page 89

Hildy Johnson Reporter protagonist of Ben Hecht and Charles MacArthur's play *The Front Page* (1925). Perhaps the archetypical fictional journalist who will do anything for a story, regardless of the effects of publicity on the people he writes about.

Page 90

policemen were using squadrols. . . . The Summerdale Scandal. In 1960, several Chicago police officers from the Summerdale District were convicted of burglary when Richard Morrison, "the babbling burglar," turned state's evidence. The cops involved stole while in uniform and on duty. An Outfit hitman later shot and wounded Morrison outside of the Cook County Courthouse at 26th and California. Algren sees the scandal as a mere reflection of the depth of Chicago's official corruption, and hence comically characterizes Chicago's response as more worry about jobs than actual moral outrage.

Page 94

Another novel The Man With the Golden Arm.

a presentation . . . Frank Sinatra Otto Preminger's 1955 film version of *The Man With the Golden Arm,* starring Frank Sinatra, Eleanor Parker, and Kim Novak. To call this film an abomination would be an understatement; Preminger and his screenwriter Walter Newman completely reverse Algren's depiction of Frankie Machine and his world. The film was a *cause celebre* for its depiction of addiction and its jazz score, but helped to blight Algren's reputation by associating his masterpiece with the pop genre of drug exposé fiction.

"I belong to. . . ." Line 14 of Walt Whitman's "You Felons on Trial in Courts."

Page 95

"Each man's death. . . ." From John Donne's *Meditation 17.*

"While there is a soul. . . ." One of Debs's most famous statements. In its entirety, it reads: "While there is a lower class I am in it, while there is a criminal element I am of it, and while there is a soul in prison I am not free." These words sum up Algren's firmest beliefs.

Tribune cartoon Newspapers often printed political cartoons on the front page; the *Tribune*'s cartoons were noted for their virulent conservatism.

Page 98

Dalton Trumbo Blacklisted Hollywood screenwriter, one of the Hollywood Ten who refused to cooperate with the HUAC and so was jailed and blacklisted.

Acknowledgments

Nothing is created in a vacuum, and we owe many great debts for assistance received in the course of this project. In particular, we would like to thank the following people for their help (published, conversational, or personal): Mark Anderson, Kim Ataide, Henry Binford, John Blades, Marc Blottner, Kasia Boddy, Carla Cappetti, Clay Cerny, Jeremy Cleveland, Thomas Cox, Bettina Drew, Perry Duis, Frederic Dumas, John Erlanger, Lawrence Evans, Liam Ford, Nina Gaspich, James Giles, Elva Griffiths, Steve Hardman, Kenan Heise, John Kass, Liam Kennedy, Rick Kogan, Richard Lalich, Warren Leming, James Lewin, John Lillig, Stuart McCarrell and the Nelson Algren Committee, Philip McGowan, John Musial, Toshiro Nakajima, Ian Peddie, Alice Prus, Jeff Rice, Carlo Rotella, Char Sandstrom, William Savage Sr., Mary and Eugene Schmittgens Sr., Daniel Simon, Carl Smith, Judith Sobiesk, John Susman, Studs Terkel, Stephen Wade, Matt Walter, Robert Ward, and Richard Westley. Special thanks go to Maggie Hivnor, Mark Bennett, and everyone at the University of Chicago Press. Finally, this edition would not exist were it not for our students at St. Ignatius College Prep, Northwestern University, and the Newberry Library.

Publishing History

The first version of *Chicago: City on the Make* hit the newsstands in the Chicago-themed October 1951 issue of the travel magazine *Holiday*. Among essays by Carl Sandburg, Gwendolyn Brooks, and Robert M. Hutchins—and civic boosterism by Robert R. McCormick, Albert Halper, Irv Kupcinet, and others—Algren's vision of Chicago stood out. The editors entitled it "One Man's Chicago," to account for its dark tone and Art Shay's starkly evocative photography of a Chicago few tourists would ever visit.

Algren substantially revised the article—which he believed had been butchered by the magazine's editors—for book publication later that same year. In an added preface (now the Afterword) to the second edition in 1961, Algren extended his argument and commented on the book's initial reception and its cultural milieu. The third edition featured photographs by Stephen Deutch and included the satiric poem, "Ode to Lower Finksville" as an epilogue. A variant of the third edition exists, because Algren wished to title his poem, "Ode to Kissassville: Or, Gone on the Arfy-Darfy," but the publisher balked. They finally agreed to publish a limited run of 100 copies with the poem so-titled. Algren died in 1981, and the fourth edition of *Chicago: City on the Make*, with Studs Terkel's Introduction, appeared in 1983.

Bibliography

We used two sorts of published texts in our research: books which were available to Algren when he wrote *Chicago: City on the Make*, and material subsequently published. Often, a turn of phrase, an image, or an unusual characterization made it clear to us that Algren had read a certain book: here, we list these first. Regarding sources not yet published when Algren wrote *City on the Make*, in most cases, the title of the book will make clear which of our annotations made use of the particular source.

Algren's Sources

Ahern, M. L. *The Political History of Chicago*. Chicago: Donohue & Henneberry, 1886.

Asbury, Herbert. *Gem of the Prairie*. New York: Alfred A. Knopf, 1940.

Bright, John. *Hizzoner Big Bill Thompson: An Idyll of Chicago*. New York: Jonathan Cape and Harrison Smith, 1930.

David, Henry. *The History of the Haymarket Affair*. New York: Russell and Russell, 1936.

Harris, Frank. *The Bomb*. New York: self-published, 1920.

Lait, Jack, and Lee Mortimer. *Chicago Confidential*. New York: Crown, 1950.

Lewis, Lloyd, and Henry Justin Smith. *Chicago: The History of its Reputation*. New York: Harcourt, Brace and Co., 1929.

Masters, Edgar Lee. *A Tale of Chicago*. New York: G. P. Putnam's Sons, 1933.

Mencken, H. L. "The Literary Capital of the United States." In *On American Books*, edited by Francis Hackett. New York: B. W. Huebsch, 1920.

Pierce, Bessie Louise. *A History of Chicago*. 3 vols. New York: Alfred A. Knopf, 1937–57.

Poole, Ernest. *Giants Gone: Men who Made Chicago*. New York: McGraw-Hill, 1943.

Sandburg, Carl. *The Chicago Race Riots: July 1919*. New York: Harcourt, Brace and Row, 1919.

Smith, Henry Justin. *Chicago: A Portrait*. New York: Century Co., 1931.

Stead, William T. *If Christ Came to Chicago*. Chicago: Laird & Lee, 1894.

Wendt, Lloyd, and Herman Kogan. *Lords of the Levee: The Story of Bathhouse John and Hinky Dink*. New York: Garden City, 1943.

Whitman, Walt. *The Portable Walt Whitman*, ed. Mark Van Doren. New York: Penguin, 1945, 1977.

Zorbaugh, Harvey W. *The Gold Coast and the Slum*. Chicago: University of Chicago Press, 1929.

Other Sources

Aherns, Art, and Eddie Gold. *Day by Day in Chicago Cubs History*. West Point, N.Y.: Leisure Press, 1982.

Asinof, Eliot. *Eight Men Out: The Black Sox and the 1919 World Series*. New York: Henry Holt, 1963.

Baudelaire, Charles. *The Complete Verse of Baudelaire, Vol. I*. Edited and translated by Francis Scarfe. London: Anvil Press Poetry, 1986.

Beauharnais v. Illinois. Available from http://lawbooksusa.com/cconlaw/beauharnaisvillinois.htm.

Boyer, Dwight. *Ghost Ships of the Great Lakes*. Cleveland: Freshwater Press, 1968.

Bukowski, Douglas. *Big Bill Thompson, Chicago, and the Politics of Image*. Urbana, Ill.: University of Illinois Press, 1998.

Cappetti, Carla. *Writing Chicago: Modernism, Ethnography and the Novel*. New York: Columbia University Press, 1993.

Christensen, Daphne, ed. *Chicago Public Works: A History*. Chicago: Rand McNally & Company, 1973.

Cohen, Adam, and Elizabeth Taylor. *American Pharoah: Richard Daley, His Battle for Chicago and the Nation*. New York: Little Brown, 2000.

Danckers, Ulrich, Jane Meredith, John F. Swenson, and Helen H. Tanner. *A Compendium of the Early History of Chicago to the Year 1835 when the Indians Left*. River Forest, Ill.: Early Chicago, Inc., 2000.

Dedmon, Emmet. *Fabulous Chicago*. New York: Random House, 1953.

Demaris, Ovid. *Captive City: Chicago in Chains*. New York: Lyle Stuart, Inc., 1969.

Drake, St. Clair and Horace R. Cayton. *Black Metropolis*. Chicago: University of Chicago Press, 1993.

Duis, Perry. *Challenging Chicago: Coping with Everyday Life, 1837–1920*. Urbana, Ill.: University of Illinois Press, 1998.

———. *The Saloon: Public Drinking in Chicago and Boston, 1880–1920*. Urbana, Ill.: University of Illinois Press, 1983.

Farr, Finis. *Chicago: A Personal History of America's Most American City*. New Rochelle, N.Y.: Arlington House, 1973.

Garraty, John A., and Mark C. Carnes, eds. *American National Biography*. New York: Oxford University Press, 1999.

Green, Paul M., and Melvin G. Holli, eds. *The Mayors: The Chicago Political Tradition*. Carbondale, Ill.: Southern Illinois University Press, 1987.

Grosch, Anthony. "H. L. Mencken and Literary Chicago," *Chicago History* 14, no. 2 (1985): pp. 4–21.

Heise, Kenan, and Ed Baumann. *Chicago Originals: A Cast of the City's Colorful Characters*. Expanded and updated edition. Chicago: Bonus Books, 1995.

Hill, Libby. *The Chicago River: A Natural and Unnatural History*. Chicago: Lake Claremont Press, 2000.

Johnson, Curt, and R. Craig Sautter. *The Wicked City: Chicago from Kenna to Capone*. Chicago: Da Capo Press, 1999.

Kenney, William Howland. *Chicago Jazz: A Cultural History, 1904–1930*. New York: Oxford University Press, 1993.

Kogan, Herman, and Rick Kogan. *Yesterday's Chicago*. Miami: E.A. Seemann Publishing, Inc, 1976.

Kogan, Herman, and Lloyd Wendt. *Chicago: A Pictorial History*. New York: Bonanza Books, 1953.

Lemann, Nicholas. *The Promised Land: The Great Black Migration and How it Changed America*. New York: Vintage, 1992.

Lind, Alan R. *Chicago Surface Lines: An Illustrated History*. Park Forest, Ill.: Transport History Press, 1974.

Lindberg, Richard C. *Chicago by Gaslight: A History of Chicago's Netherworld, 1880–1920*. Chicago: Academy Chicago Publishers, 1996.

———. *Return to the Scene of the Crime. A Guide to Infamous Places in Chicago*. Nashville: Cumberland House, 1999.

———. *To Serve and Collect: Chicago Politics and Police Corruption from the Lager Beer Riot to the Summerdale Scandal, 1955–1960*. Carbondale, Ill.: Southern Illinois University Press, 1991.

Lowe, David. *Lost Chicago*. Boston: Houghton Mifflin, 1975.

McPhaul, John J. *Deadlines and Monkeyshines: The Fabled World of Chicago Journalism*. Englewood Cliffs, N.J.: Prentice-Hall, 1962.

Rotella, Carlo. *October Cities: The Redevelopment of Urban Literature*. Berkeley: University of California Press, 1998.

Royko, Mike. *Boss: Richard J. Daley of Chicago*. New York: Dutton, 1971.

Skilnik, Bob. *The History of Beer and Brewing in Chicago, 1833–1978*. St. Paul: Pogo Press, 1999.

Smith, Carl. *Chicago and the American Literary Imagination*. Chicago: University of Chicago Press, 1984.

———. "The Dramas of Haymarket." On-line exhibit in collaboration between the Chicago Historical Society and Northwestern University, 2000. Available from http://www.chicagohs.org/ dramas.

———. "The Great Chicago Fire and the Web of Memory." On-line exhibit in collaboration between the Chicago Historical Society and Northwestern University, 1996. Available from http://www.chicagohs.org/fire.

———. *Urban Disorder and the Shape of Belief: The Great Chicago Fire, the Haymarket Bomb and the Model Town of Pullman.* Chicago: University of Chicago Press, 1995.

Spear, Allan H. *Black Chicago: The Making of a Negro Ghetto, 1890–1920.* Chicago: University of Chicago Press, 1967.

Starkey, David, and Richard Guzman, eds. *Smokestacks and Skyscrapers: An Anthology of Chicago Writing.* Chicago: Wild Onion Books, 1999.

Stevenson, Swanson, ed. *Chicago Days.* Wheaton, Ill.: First Cantigny Division Foundation, 1997.

Story of Chicago, in Connection with the Printing Business, The. Chicago: Regan Printing House, 1912.

Note on the Editors

DAVID SCHMITTGENS was born and raised in south suburban Park Forest. He is a longtime resident of Chicago and has degrees from Eastern Illinois University and DePaul University. He is currently a graduate student in the Master of Liberal Arts program at the University of Chicago. He also teaches a Chicago literature class at St. Ignatius College Prep, where he has been a member of the faculty since 1994.

BILL SAVAGE was born, raised, and educated in Chicago, which explains a lot of things. The son of a Chicago police officer and grandson of a sportswriter, Savage received his formal education from the Jesuits at St. Ignatius College Prep and Loyola University; his informal education from his mother and her love for all of Chicago, its alleys and boulevards, viaducts and side streets and State Street alike. He wrote his doctoral dissertation, on the evolving reputation of Nelson Algren and the ways in which aspects of material culture communicate literary values, at Northwestern University, where he currently teaches. He writes and conducts research in two distinct areas: hermeneutics, or the philosophy of textual interpretation, and twentieth-century Chicago writers. With Daniel Simon, Savage co-edited Algren's *The Man With the Golden Arm: 50th Anniversary Critical Edition* (Seven Stories Press, 1999). A lifelong resident of Rogers Park, Savage has never lived out of earshot of the El, although at the moment he prizes his thirteenth-floor view of Lake Michigan "slipping out of used colors for new."

Photographs